S.A.S. SIXTY AND SINGLE

YOUR SURVIVAL GUIDE TO DATING

FIONA LAMBERT

Synergy Publishing
Newberry, FL 32669
publishwithsynergy.com

S.A.S. Sixty and Single
By Fiona Lambert

Printed in the United Kingdom.
International Standard Book Number: ISBN 978-1-61036-914-5

Interior Layout Design:
Cris Convery
hello@crisconvery.com

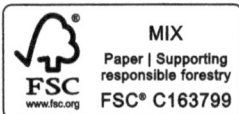

FSC
www.fsc.org

MIX
Paper | Supporting
responsible forestry
FSC® C163799

PROLOGUE

When you're single and you're over sixty
You might think dating is risky
But you'll feel so alive
And know you will thrive
As hell, you're still feeling frisky.

If you're open to go and tempt fate,
Testing out different new dates,
You'll get a big thrill
All dressed to kill,
Searching for a handsome new mate.

You love wearing just what you choose,
Ignore trolls, and all their abuse,
They'll only be jealous,
When they see all the fellas,
Forming orderly queues.

It's a myth that we are now stale,
Our sex life is going to fail?
With confidence high,
I'm not going to lie,
My next date is one lucky male!

Let's make this dating malarkey a brilliant experience.

CONTENTS

CHAPTER 1

CAN YOU BE SASSY, SINGLE AND SEXY OVER 60?

ARE YOU STILL DATEABLE?

Like my last book, if you had asked me if I would be writing about the trials and tribulations of being back on the dating market at 61, I would have laughed at the thought.
But here I am!

Several people have said how 'brave' it is to take the step to be single, uncertain about what will happen, AT MY AGE! But I chose rather than have security and lead a life that was not making me happy, to instead, own my 60s.

I will caveat what I am saying by sharing that I loved and still love my husband of 31 years, but having met when I was 23 and he was 26, we developed into different people, with different interests and goals. We decided to part ways amicably, appreciating with huge gratitude what we had had together, but recognising we wanted different futures.

My first book *Invincible not Invisible* was about turning 60 and wanting to see this milestone birthday, not as the end of my best years, but the beginning. I got to my fittest and tried lots of new experiences to prove it's never too late and you're never too old. It made me recognise that the woman I have grown into, a woman that wants a life that's extraordinary, not ordinary. Still seeking out new experiences, challenges and adventures, meant I wasn't going to settle for the easy, comfortable option for the best 1/3 of my life. I was ready to embrace change, with the risks and lows that it might bring, optimistic that ultimately I would find joy.

And I am not alone.

25% of divorces are happening when couples are over 50 with 2/3 of these being initiated by women.

WHY ARE MORE CHOOSING LATER LIFE DIVORCE?

We are living longer and don't want to compromise happiness for the rest of our lives! We want to prioritise personal happiness and self-fulfilment over conforming to society's expectations. We are living healthier lives, making it possible to enjoy vibrant, active lifestyles that don't necessarily correlate with the way our current partners choose to lead their lives.

I have several friends and acquaintances who have chosen to leave their husbands in their 50s or 60s, and this is one of the most expressed reasons.

In my previous book, *Invincible not Invisible,* one of my key drivers to getting to my fittest at 60 was I wanted to see this landmark birthday as a beginning and not a slide into a greying age. I believe myself and my friends are looking at living their best lives and seeing that their current relationship is not going to give them that. My favourite expression, 'you are never too old and it's never too late', applies to embarking on a new, single life too! It's a time for new opportunities and personal growth rather than a period focused on traditional family roles.

Women are not making this choice because they necessarily want a different partner or relationship. Society is now totally accepting of different lifestyles, including being single by choice. The idea that happiness and fulfilment can come from a variety of sources, not just from a romantic relationship, has gained widespread acceptance.

And yes, we still look great. With healthy eating and regular exercise, many of us are in even better shape than we were when we were younger. I share more about this journey—and how I reached my best shape at 60—in *Invincible Not Invisible*, for those curious to dive deeper.

We now have more treatments to offset the dreaded hormonal changes that perimenopause and menopause bring, more sophisticated skincare and health supplements, and more inspiration than ever around lifestyle, life coaching, and fashion. We also benefit from regular health checks and a greater emphasis on preventive care, helping us detect and manage age-related issues early—and stay vibrant and healthy for longer.

There should be no stigma to being single as an older woman. There should be no concern that we will be stuck on the shelf, past our sell by date. Women have more role models, incredible high-profile women, whether in the media, politics or business world, who are single and thriving, showing that it is possible to lead a fulfilling and successful life without a partner.

There are so many women that embody independence, confidence and desirability at an older age. Look at Jennifer Aniston, Susan Sarandon, Carol Vorderman, Kim Cattrall, Charlize Theron, Jane Fonda, Cher.... the list goes on.

We have a strong, female, supportive community around us. The rise of social media and online communities has created spaces where women can connect, share experiences and support each other, so there is more companionship and connection than ever before in choosing to be single.

This all makes sense, but as I know myself, it doesn't make it any easier should you decide to be single or ultimately embark on trying to find another relationship.

I'm sure I am not alone to have been thinking;

"Will I be ok on my own?"

"What am I looking for?"

"Will I be seen as too old to date?"

"How on earth do I meet someone?"

"Where do I meet someone?"

"How do I use a dating app?"

"Which are the best dating apps for me?"

"What type of men go online to date, and how can I weed out the wheat from the chaff?"

"What on earth do I wear to date?"

Have you been going over and over that list in your mind?

It sounds like a minefield, right? Boy, how different the world of dating is from when I met my husband in the mid-eighties. If you were lucky you managed to swap numbers on a piece of paper at the end of the evening, hope it was a real one and didn't lose it by the next day!

It's true, you're not as young and carefree as you were in your 20s and you may well have gathered some baggage in your 30s, but dating in later life should be so much more rewarding.

If you've been single you'll probably be receiving dating advice from everyone who thinks you want to change this status. You shouldn't feel under any pressure to jump back in.

As I reentered the dating pool myself, all of this crossed my mind. I realised there had to be a way to share thoughts on this. How about if I tried to cover all of these dilemmas, to be your guinea pig (a foxy one at that!) and report back?

I will take you through not only my research on dating apps, but also look at other ways to meet people outside of apps, which although seems so much harder now, is still very possible.

I am also going to share tips from expert matchmakers and dating stories of success and failures (or let's call them experiences) from myself and friends, for you to learn from. There will be laughter and the odd tear, but you have got to put yourself out there.

CHAPTER 2
DATE YOURSELF FIRST

For whatever reason, if you are in the same boat as me, you need to recognise that you can't change the past, you can only learn from it.

You can't predict the future, but you can walk into it head held high, if you focus on you now. Recognise you are fabulous, appreciate all the wonderful things about yourself.

You happen to be single right now, and you are going to use this time, whether it's to meet a partner, or not, to recognise just how great you are. Before I went leaping into the world of dating, I decided to start with falling in love with myself first and you should too!

Whether you've been single for a while or are recently single, whether you're broken-hearted or relieved, before embarking on another relationship take this time to date yourself.

Having been married for 31 years and in a relationship for 37, it meant I had been half of a couple for more than half of my life. In my case I recognised that in being with someone for such a long time, you lose a little of yourself. The compromises you both make to make a long term relationship survive, inevitably changes you and your behaviour, views and actions.

I realised I needed to take some time for self-reflection and awareness. To be comfortable and understand myself first, to then work out what I need from a future relationship. The first thing I needed to do was rediscover my independence. It was to be liberating and terrifying at the same time. Being single at 61 was never going to be the same as being single at 23, but I was ready to re-find my independence.

I hadn't been on a girl's holiday since I was 24, so one of the first things I did was book two holidays with friends, both with a focus on fitness and well-being, which I had never been able to do before as it wasn't my husband's choice of holiday.

I'm very impulsive, very impatient, but I told myself not to rush. Spending the time taking a step back, to ask myself questions, would allow me to make better dating decisions. I was to find out it takes a lot of resilience to keep going on fruitless dates (more on how to avoid date burnout later). I could see it would be easy to get frustrated or disheartened if you don't find 'the one' straight away. Investing the time now, will help shortcut the process and mean not investing lots of energy into dates that aren't ever going to match up to what you need.

LOVE YOURSELF

We've all heard the phrase that "the most important relationship you will ever have is with yourself," and it's true.

In the journey to finding love, self-love is the fundamental foundation of a healthy, fulfilling relationship. In this section we will explore why self-love is crucial in dating, the ways in which you can improve your relationship with yourself and how embracing it can transform your romantic life.

Investing the time in rediscovering and falling in love with yourself first, will give you the confidence to know who you are, what you deserve. It will give you the power to say no rather than yes to dates that aren't right.

WHAT IS SELF-LOVE AND WHY DOES IT MATTER?

Self-love is about valuing and caring for yourself and ultimately loving who you are and everything that makes you, you. It means accepting your flaws and strengths, setting boundaries and prioritising your own well-being. When you practice self-love, you recognise your worth and refuse to settle for less than you deserve. Isn't that what we all want when it comes to dating?

Self-love plays a vital role in your dating journey because it brings out the best version of you in the best possible way. Self-love breeds confidence. When you know your worth, you are less likely to settle for an unhealthy relationship. Confidence attracts the right partners and sets the tone for mutual respect and admiration in a relationship.

Not only that but understanding and respecting your own needs helps you set boundaries within the relationship. Healthy boundaries ensure that your relationship is balanced and that both partners' needs are met. This prevents co-dependency and fosters mutual respect. You don't need someone to complete you, you should be a complete human by yourself. Someone can then compliment what you already have, by joining you as a partner in life.

When you love yourself, you are also better equipped to love others. Often those that do not see their own self-worth, struggle to let their guard down and let others in because they don't understand what that other person could possibly see in them. Self-love allows you to be emotionally available, which is essential for a deep, meaningful connection. It helps you communicate your feelings honestly and openly and allows you to experience every new relationship with a blank slate and solid foundation on which you can both build.

HOW TO CULTIVATE SELF-LOVE

Self-care is a practical way to show yourself love. This can be as simple as taking time for a hobby, exercising, enjoying a pamper session or simply ensuring you get enough rest. Regular self-care boosts your mood and helps maintain your overall well-being, which in turn, I guarantee, will have a positive effect on your life.

And while self-care covers many aspects including physical, emotional and mental self-care activities, don't forget to also pay attention to how you speak to yourself. Your inner dialogue significantly impacts your self-esteem. Replace negative self-talk with affirmations and positive statements. Remind yourself daily of your strengths and achievements and eventually you won't have to 'fake it 'til you make it', because you'll realise just how amazing you are.

Finally, remember to forgive yourself. Everyone makes mistakes. Holding onto past mistakes can hinder your ability to not only love yourself but also to move on from them onto newer and brighter opportunities. Practice self-forgiveness and understand that mistakes are part of growth – that includes relationships and dates too! Every date or relationship is a journey. The key lies in what you take from it. So, whether you've come out of an unhealthy relationship, or you had a disastrous date, don't worry. Listen to what the experience taught you and forgive yourself as that will allow you to close the door on that chapter and start afresh with someone who deserves everything you have to offer.

THE IMPACT OF SELF-LOVE ON RELATIONSHIPS

When you practice self-love, you emit positive energy that attracts like-minded individuals. If you are confident, set healthy boundaries and appreciate all the unique traits that make who you are, you are more likely to meet partners who respect and value you.

Relationships flourish when both partners are secure and confident in themselves, and it is one of the most common traits that someone looks for in a partner. After all, self-love leads to healthier communication, deeper emotional connection, and overall relationship satisfaction.

Self-love also helps in reducing insecurities and anxiety within a relationship. When you are confident in yourself, you trust your partner more, leading to a more stable and loving relationship. And who wouldn't want that?

Self-love is not a luxury; it's a necessity in the dating world. It sets the stage for healthier, more fulfilling relationships and leads you to understanding who you are and the type of person that you would like to settle down with. By prioritising self-love, you enhance your dating experience, attract the right partners, and build lasting, meaningful connections.

Take the first step towards a healthier love life by embracing self-love. Remember, the journey to finding the right partner begins with the most important relationship of all, the one with yourself.

How you talk to yourself is everything and it's easy to listen to the inner critic.

"I always date the wrong type"

"I'm too old"

"I have too many 'saggy bits'"

"I've forgotten how to flirt"

"I'm scared of getting hurt"

If you start off by thinking these things they have a tendency to happen! Thinking negative thoughts attracts negative experiences.

It's called having limiting beliefs, so we need to ditch that inner critic and instead talk to ourselves like our best friend is giving us a pep talk!

As I ventured upon this journey I decided to focus on the plus points of dating in later life.

YOU ARE A CATCH!

Celebrate what *you* bring to the next relationship you have. Be the best, happiest version of you and only give that to someone who meets your needs and desires.

These are things I did. Try it. Let's start off by celebrating why you are such a fabulous person to date.

"How are you going to love somebody, if you don't love yourself?" RuPaul

Fill in the box below and it **has to be at least 5 things,** I hope it's a long list!

I am a fabulous person to date because...

Now stand in front of the mirror and read this list out loud to yourself.

Really mean it. Really appreciate what a wonderful catch you will be for someone.

I hope you're feeling confident, glowing, filled with self respect and most importantly smiling!

Your mindset is going to be key to make this the best time of your life, whether you are single, looking for a relationship or in one.

When you appreciate yourself and all your loveable qualities, you will radiate positivity that attracts like-minded people. If you are confident, appreciating all the unique traits that make who you are, you are more likely to meet someone who respects and values you.

Ok, so now's the time to be sure about who you are. To be the most authentic, datable, desirable version of yourself. When you come to write your dating profile, this section will pay dividends.

PERSONALITY

How would you, or your best friends and family describe you? Make it positive!

VALUES

Think about the values that are most important to you. This could include honesty, compassion, loyalty or a shared sense of adventure.

LIFESTYLE

Consider your current lifestyle. Are you active and adventurous, or do you prefer quiet, home-based activities?

INTERESTS

What hobbies do you have or activities do you do? Would you like those interests shared? Or do you just want ensure you have enough of your own time to enjoy them?

LIFE STAGE

At this stage in life, authenticity is crucial. Be honest with yourself and your goals. What do you want from the future? When it comes to location, how far are you willing to travel to meet? Do you want monogamy? To play the field? Maintain independence?

STRENGTHS

An ideal partner should complement your strengths and you may like them to be able to support you in areas you don't excel or enjoy.

	Try to write at least 5-10	Now edit your top 3
PERSONALITY		
VALUES		
LIFESTYLE		
INTERESTS		
LIFE STAGE		

CHAPTER 3
DEFINE YOUR IDEAL PARTNER

Do you remember playing Mr Potato Head? Or maybe you had a book where you could flip divided pages over to make up a person using the head, middle and legs of your choice?

Well let's try to create our perfect partner profile and see how close we can get to that!

Let's start by listing what you bring to a relationship.

Wow – this is why you are an absolute dream partner! You shouldn't be settling for any less than you deserve so let's find someone that deserves you.

You've acknowledged what an amazing catch you are but what do you want a relationship to bring?

As you start to answer this question, the answers might be companionship, someone to share experiences with.

If these are top of your list, consider; are these just ways to not feel lonely, that could equally be achieved spending time with friends and family?

If you have a chance with a clean slate to find a new partner do you not want them to enrich your life and bring out the best in you and in turn you to bring out the best in them?

List below the ways your ideal partner would complement your life.

As I said, you can't change the past, but you can learn from it.

If you have come out of a serious relationship (or two) in the past, or even been married before, there's a reason why your ex is, well, your ex! You don't want to fall into the same trap this time around so let's evaluate it.

In previous relationships;

WHAT WORKED WELL?	
WHAT DIDN'T?	
WHAT WERE THE ATTRACTIVE QUALITIES	
WHAT WERE THE THINGS THAT IRRITATED YOU?	

Are there any repeating patterns to note?

We often go for a type and if you have relationships that never seem to work out, think about the things you will not accept in your next relationship. What you get, is what you tolerate.

A few of my own examples are;

- I won't accept poor communication
- I won't date someone that can't accept me for the passionate, driven, boisterous me
- I won't accept inconsistent behaviour

This really helped me as I started the process of dating, as if they were really poor in replying with messages, and good communication is key for me, I could point it out and if things didn't change, I would be able to see that this person wasn't for me.

List what you won't accept below – make it at least 4 or 5 points.

What won't I accept in my next relationship?

SO YOU SPENT SOME TIME THINKING ABOUT YOURSELF.

You know how fabulous you are. You've a really clear picture of what you like about yourself and what you bring to a relationship.

Now it's time to think about what you'd like in a partner and for your future.

This doesn't have to be set in stone, and you should definitely be open to being flexible throughout the process, but it is also the case that some things in life are completely non-negotiable. For example, have you got children, or do you want to find someone who has children? Are you looking for someone who might want to get married someday or are you looking for someone who just wants fun? It's important that you have some idea of what you're looking for before you begin the search.

Here's some thoughts, as a good place to start;

Personality What character traits do you find attractive? How would you want to describe their personality?

Values You know your values, do you look for the same? But as you are now considering what you want from a relationship, what would your ideal partner value?

Lifestyle Consider your current lifestyle. Are you active and adventurous, or do you prefer quiet, home-based activities? How would you like someone to fit into that?

Interests What hobbies do you have or activities do you do? Would you like those interests shared? Or do you need to ensure you have enough of your own time to enjoy them?

Life stage You're clear on your goals, what you want from the future. What about theirs? When it comes to location, how far are you willing to travel to meet?

Strengths An ideal partner should complement your strengths and you may like them to be able to support you in areas you don't excel or enjoy.

Relationship type Monogamous, open, casual? The choice is yours.

	Try to write at least 5–10	Non-negotiables	Flexible
PERSONALITY			
VALUES			
LIFESTYLE			
INTERESTS			
LIFE STAGE			
STRENGTHS			
RELATIONSHIP TYPE			

NOW PRIORITIZE YOUR LIST INTO THE TOP 5.

Decide which 5 qualities from your list overall are truly non-negotiable. This will help you focus on what's important. It will help you navigate choices as you enter the dating world again.

NON-NEGOTIABLES

STAY OPEN-MINDED.

I decided I needed to be open to meeting people who didn't necessarily meet all my criteria. After all, I was cognisant that my own profile only reflected a very small part of me. Naturally impulsive and normally quite intuitive about people, I was open to meeting people who may not fit the exact criteria but could still be a great match.

Everyone has their quirks and there's no sense being with someone if you want to change big parts of their personality. You wouldn't want to be with someone who tried to do that to you. So it's important to keep an open mind when meeting new people; don't get stuck on your 'shopping list' of what makes a perfect partner, otherwise you set your expectations too high and more often than not, no one will ever tick every box and you will be disappointed. I started off with a minimum height of 6ft and an age bracket of 47–58. I had an interesting chat with a virtual stranger who had seen I had started internet dating and was frustrated by the views cast upon older women, for dating younger men. She said how she was three years into a relationship with a man 15 years younger than her. She advised me not to let society or my own biases restrict my thinking or dictate what was an appropriate age gap.

Sometimes, unexpected connections can be the most rewarding. No one is perfect, and it's important to be realistic about your expectations. Knowing my non-negotiables and things I was flexible about meant I stayed open to more possibilities.

CHAPTER 4
WHICH DATING APP IS FOR YOU?

So you've dated yourself and you've decided what you want from a partner. You're feeling ready to start the online dating experience!

So which app is for you?

For me, with so many dating apps available, deciding which one to choose felt overwhelming. My friends had views on some, and I had preconceptions about others.

Each app offered something a bit different, had a different style and preferences. In the interest of research, I tried 6 that were recommended. All of them had a free version but the filters or choices were radically limited, so to make it worthwhile I paid to upgrade the type of membership I had, to see how they worked fully. Watch out for the auto renew on subscriptions if you test them out, otherwise it can end up expensive.

I have to say the difference between using a dating app in a big city like London or Manchester, is a very different experience to using it in a sleepier town or village due to the number of people who match your criteria in a radius. The quieter your location, the broader you may have to extend your criteria to make the algorithm work for you.

I started with men over 6ft and over 46 years old. I ended up changing to over 5ft 10in and over 42! Be prepared to flex.

BUMBLE

The first one I tried and on which I probably had most success.

I started on Bumble as the first recommendation from a girlfriend. Bumble's success is its unique approach to online dating. It allows only women to initiate conversations in heterosexual matches, so it stands out in the crowded field of dating apps. I would recommend this if you want quality over quantity and to feel more in control of this odd experience called online dating!

Pros

The power is in your hands!
Women initiate the conversation, making the first move in heterosexual matches, reducing unwanted messages and making you feel more in control. This design helps to shift traditional dating dynamics. My matchmaker friend has a theory that this slightly emasculates men, but I didn't find it meant a shortage of matches.

Safe
Bumble has a reputation for prioritising user safety. I would highly recommend features like photo verification. I tried briefly without it on, and there were men using fake photos to lure women in, alongside claiming to do jobs that made them seem reliable or kind. Who else would feel a tug on the heartstrings for a paediatric surgeon, taking time out to chat on Bumble from saving children's lives? He was also very handsome, but when, feeling suspicious, I reverse searched his photo, it was actually a photo of an Argentinian porn star. If it feels too good to be true, trust your instincts you're right. There are guidelines to prevent inappropriate behaviour and create a safer online space compared to some other dating apps. You can easily block or report profiles if they make you feel uncomfortable.

24 hour call to action
Unlike apps that foster endless swiping, with Bumble you have to engage quickly. Matches disappear after 24 hours if no message is sent, creating a sense of urgency and it discourages superficial matching.

Connections other than dating
Not that I joined for this, but Bumble isn't just for romance. With its Bumble BFF and Bumble Bizz modes, the app can also help those looking for friendships or professional networking.

Can switch to travel mode or have temporary pauses

If you are travelling, you could put on your destination as you travelled or knowing where you'd be in a day or two to meet matches. I found when in London, there were a lot of men from overseas on business, or from long distances away within the UK who were looking for a match as they travelled. If you are looking for more than just intimacy without commitment or uninterested in fun, casual dates it's worth taking extra time to see where they are actually from, so as not to waste your time.

User-friendly

Bumble has a sleek, simple, intuitive design that makes it stress free to use. Its straightforward navigation makes it easy to set up and use, even for those less familiar with technology.

Quality of matches

Whether it's the women first approach, or Bumble's emphasis on safety and respect, it seemed to attract a higher percentage of men looking for more meaningful connections. The overall quality of matches seems to be higher compared to other apps with a more casual focus.

Cons

Pressure on women to initiate

So I appreciated the opportunity to take control, but some of you may find the responsibility of initiating conversations stressful. For men who join this app, this structure can be frustrating if their matches don't send the first message within the 24-hour window.

Limited time to act

Whilst it stops endless, unthought through swiping, Bumble's 24-hour time limit for initiating conversations can be a double-edged sword. While it promotes active engagement, it does mean unless you are on the app regularly, it can lead to missed opportunities. If you're time pressured and busy this may be an issue for you.

Subscription costs

While Bumble does offer a free version, many desirable features, like extending matches or seeing who has swiped right on your profile, are locked behind a paid subscription. I went for this as finding out people who liked you seemed a more sure fire way of matching. There are big discounts for subscribing for a longer term but you have to decide how long do you really anticipate being on it?

Superficial matching

Like most dating apps, Bumble relies on swiping based on profile pictures and short bios, which can lead to superficial decisions. When you create your bio, you can only choose 5 words from a list of around 250 likes, interests and character traits. Mine for example were positivity, theatre, dancing, design and TV dramas. You get matched based on one common like e.g. dancing. This design may not appeal to you if you're seeking deeper connections from the outset.

Location

Bumble reacts to where you are so if you are travelling on the train to London from Leicester as I was, I got matches at every point on the journey. If you don't want this to happen you have to change your settings.

Same profiles liking you

Not sure if it's because I used Bumble more than any other app, but I had several men like me several times despite me swiping right. They were either persistent or the app somehow allowed this to happen. In some cases they came up as 'New Here' so I assume they had re-set up their profiles.

Accidentally super swiping!

The layout of the app meant that sometimes as I swiped right, I accidentally hit the super swipe button meaning I looked, unintentionally, extra keen.

TINDER

I was reluctant to go on Tinder with a presumption it was for more casual hook-ups. But after speaking to friends, they advised me that preferences meant you could match with men with more long term intentions. Its right swipe/left swipe action allows you to quickly decide if you're interested in someone. However, for me I found its profiles too superficial and the sheer numbers quite daunting, but read on for more detail and it may be for you if you want to experiment.

Pros

Easy to use
Tinder's simple swipe-left or swipe-right action is intuitive and user-friendly, so easy if you're new to dating apps. Creating a profile takes only a few minutes, so you can jump into the experience almost instantly.

Large number of users
Tinder's popularity means it has lots of potential matches from across the globe. This increases the likelihood of finding someone who matches your preferences, whether you're looking for casual dating, friendships, or a serious relationship.

Geolocation feature
The app uses geolocation to match users with others nearby, making it practical for finding local connections. Interestingly, out of 3500 men who had liked me, when I narrowed it down to people nearby, who had a bio and a verified profile, I only came across 3! This feature could be useful for people who have recently moved to a new city or are travelling.

Choice around intentions
Despite my pre-conceptions, Tinder does cater to a wide range of users, from those seeking serious relationships to those looking for casual encounters. You are going to come across diverse individuals, so put the right filters in and you may match with someone who has the same goals as you.

Enhanced features with Tinder Plus/Gold
If you're willing to pay for premium services, Tinder Plus and Tinder Gold offer features like unlimited swipes, the ability to see who has liked your profile, and Passport, which allows you to match with people in different cities or countries. I tried Tinder Gold in order to see who had liked me, as the scale of numbers was too hard to navigate and this was one way of narrowing it down.

Cons

Superficial matching
Tinder is very image-based, with users making decisions based on a few photos and a short and superficial bio. Men are already very image focussed, so this app feels even more so than others, that women are judged more on appearance than personality.

Large number of users
A plus and a minus! The large user base can also be a drawback, whether it's you trying to find someone but also from trying to stand out from the competition. In major cities, profiles can feel like an endless stream, making it hard to really look at profiles in depth. As a woman, it makes it difficult to stand out so you have to make your profile particularly attractive or unique.

Time-consuming
The swiping process can become addictive, the sheer numbers mean you can spend excessive time on the app without necessarily achieving meaningful connections. It can start to feel like a bit of a game, a chore or a bit of a waste of time.

Such a mixed bag of people
While Tinder offers opportunities for all types of relationships, this means it also has the biggest mix of odd balls, chancers, curious, casual and then very occasionally a good match. This can deter users seeking long-term commitments, as they might encounter many people who don't share their intentions.

Catfishing and fake profiles
As with many online platforms, Tinder is not immune to fake profiles and catfishing, but the sheer numbers and superficial profiles make it easier for them to use this platform. Be on your guard!

Cost of premium features
While Tinder is free to use, its premium features, like most apps, come at a cost. For some, the monthly subscription fees for Tinder Plus or Gold may feel excessive, especially if they don't use the app frequently and still find the sieving for gold process too difficult.

HINGE

Hinge was another popular choice with friends due to its focus on fostering meaningful relationships. Unlike swipe-heavy apps like Tinder, Hinge places emphasis on helping users connect on a deeper level through thoughtful prompts, detailed profiles, and mutual interests. If you want to get to know more about someone from an online profile and focus on local, this is for you.

Pros

Focus on meaningful connections

Of all of the apps I tried, the extensive profile setup had more revealing questions which allowed for some fun and personality to come through. Hinge differentiates itself by encouraging you to engage in conversations that go beyond surface-level interactions. Profiles include prompts such as "Two truths and a lie" or "I'm overly competitive about..." that spark creativity and make for a genuine conversation. It has voice and video notes options on profile. This design encourages users to focus on compatibility rather than just physical attraction.

Detailed profiles

On Hinge, you have to fill out more detailed information compared to other apps. In addition to basic demographic data, you can list your education, job, religious beliefs, political leanings, and even preferred drinking or smoking habits. These features make it easier to filter out people who might not be your type.

Most compatible matches

Hinge's algorithm prioritises presenting you with "Most Compatible" matches daily. This feature aims to pair you based on shared values, behaviours, and interests, increasing the likelihood of forming meaningful connections. I have to say I didn't find this very effective for me maybe because my location had a less dense population and matches were limited.

Interactive features

Hinge helps interaction by allowing you to like specific parts of a profile, such as photos or answers to prompts, instead of simply swiping. You can focus on individual aspects you find appealing, making the connection feel more personalised.

Setting preferences

With an upgraded membership, the app allows for fine-tuning preferences, including age range, distance, and even specifics like height or religious views, offering you more control over the matching experience. For this reason I found this app the best if you wanted to find someone local to you.

Cons

Subscription costs

While the free version of Hinge offers many features, premium subscriptions (Hinge Preferred) unlock key tools, such as unlimited likes, advanced filters, and seeing who liked your profile. It was quite pricey, so unless you're serious about committing to online dating, this may put you off.

Time-intensive setup

Creating a Hinge profile does require more time and effort compared to apps like Bumble or Tinder, which only ask for basic information. Although this has benefits you might find this process cumbersome or off-putting.

Limited daily likes

If you use Hinge for free, you are restricted to a limited number of likes per day, which can be frustrating if you want to connect with more people. This feature is trying to push you towards purchasing the premium plan.

Quality of matches can vary

Despite its algorithm, I found inconsistency in the quality of matches. I wasn't sure if this was driven by my location and lack of potential matches.

ELITE SINGLES

Elite's dating app seemed appealing as more niche, and promised to connect ambitious, educated, and career-driven singles looking for meaningful relationships. Despite finding one great match, it seemed very much to match me solely on age with elderly men!

Pros

Targeted audience

One of the main appeals of the Elite dating app was its focus on a specific demographic. It's designed for individuals who are educated, ambitious and have successful careers. It's one of the pricier apps so you have to have the money to invest in it. It filters its user base, making it more likely to find a compatible match among people with shared values, goals and lifestyles.

Quality over quantity

Elite has a selective admission process, where you have to meet certain criteria, such as holding a degree or working in prestigious industries. This ensures that you interact with profiles that align with your expectations.

Advanced matching algorithms

The application process asked lots of very different questions that covered anything from lifestyle to how organised you were, from interests through to art preferences, from how your friend describes you to your musical taste. The algorithms then try to pair individuals based on their professional backgrounds, education, and personal preferences, giving a score on how many things you match on. The selection process minimises time spent scrolling through lots of incompatible profiles.

Cons

Limited matches
While targeting a specific audience, and with sophisticated algorithms this means a smaller pool of potential matches. For me, in a less populated part of the UK and at 61, I got very few matches and was only sent men of 65–70 as potential suitors that they had matched with me. At 61 I seemed to be very much judged by my age on Elite more than any other app.

Exclusivity makes it restrictive
While exclusivity is a selling point, it's also a drawback. The stringent admission process might exclude individuals who don't meet specific educational or career criteria, even if they could be a compatible match, so there are no wild cards!

Expensive
Elite does come with a premium price tag, reflecting their targeted niche market and user base. Subscription fees are steep compared to other dating apps, making it less accessible if you're on a budget.

Extensive application process
The vetting process for joining the Elite was lengthy and very detailed. While this ensures quality, if you aren't very patient this will seem very time consuming.

MILLIONAIRE MATCH

As someone who has had a successful career, a couple of dates I went on found my business success and intellect intimidating. Based on this, my friend suggested I try 'Millionaire Match'. It's a niche dating app tailored to affluent singles and those interested in connecting with them. Its focus is on high-net-worth professionals, celebrities, and individuals seeking meaningful relationships. I tried it for a month to test. Due to being niche, it had very few matches, and sadly they certainly weren't of the calibre I expected. It seemed to be very USA based. If you want to find a millionaire in the USA, this is the app for you!

Pros

Targeted audience

Millionaire Match purports to have a highly specific user base. It caters exclusively to wealthy individuals or those aspiring to connect with them. This targeting eliminates the guesswork and appeals to people who value financial success and stability in a partner. You expect profiles that align with your preferences, saving time and effort.

Premium features and verification

Millionaire Match verifies its users. Wealthy members can prove their income levels through documentation, which enhances trust and reduces the likelihood of encountering fake profiles.

Exclusive experience

If you pay for premium, the app provides a high-end dating experience, offering unique features such as luxury date ideas, access to premium events, and a concierge service. If you have the cash, add a touch of sophistication to users' interactions.

Tailored matching options

Millionaire Match welcomes members from diverse professional backgrounds, including entrepreneurs, doctors, lawyers, and celebrities. If you want to be very specific, you can connect with a range of individuals, broadening your opportunities to a perfect match.

Cons

High membership cost

The exclusivity of Millionaire Match comes with a price. There is a free version, but access to premium features, and you need them, such as sending unlimited messages, advanced search filters and priority profile placement all require a subscription. As it's targeting an affluent audience, this doesn't come cheap.

Inconsistency

Free membership, and how the algorithm worked meant a lot of men who tried to match with me weren't professionals who met the criteria. Oddly on peoples' profiles you can read comments, and there were certainly plenty of people making comments on profiles, both men and women, who were just after a sugar mummy or daddy.

Risk of superficial connections

Given the app's focus on wealth and financial stability, it's possible for a match where the priority is material attributes over emotional or personal compatibility. This wasn't why I did it, but I could see how it could happen. It may be that's what you want.

Niche market

While Millionaire Match's exclusivity is good for its target audience, it also limits its user base. This niche appeal certainly didn't come up with many options for me unless they were in Europe or the USA.

RAYA

Much as I'd like to review Raya, despite applying to join in April, at the time of writing this, seven months on, I am still on a waiting list. I have a significant social media following, a successful career history in fashion retail and do public speaking, so in theory should be a good candidate. I have seven recommendations from people I know who are on it.

So why have I not been accepted? Turns out that it has a 7% acceptance rate. A 500 strong community vet you and I am not deemed good enough!

I do suspect age has something to do with it, as they look at what is needed for their database and I know at 61, I will not be everyone's ideal partner. I have had feedback that due to the niche nature of the membership, many on the platform are vain or arrogant.

I decided if I am not good enough for them, they are not good enough for me and have hit delete on the app.

MY CONCLUSION

Navigating the dating app landscape at 40, 50 or indeed 61, can be challenging but also fun and rewarding. Each app has its strengths and weaknesses, the best choice will depend on your individual preferences and dating goals. Whether seeking casual companionship or a serious relationship, I hope understanding the pros and cons I found of each platform will help you make an informed decision, enhance the online dating experience and short cut the process.

	Potential Matches available	Personalised for your needs	Value for money	Ease of use	Safety
BUMBLE	★★★★★	★★★★	★★★★	★★★★	★★★★★
TINDER	★★★★★	★★★	★★★	★★★★	★★★
HINGE	★★★	★★★★	★★	★★★	★★★
ELITE SINGLES	★★	★★★★	★	★★★	★★★★
MILLIONAIRE MATCH	★	★	★	★★	★★★
RAYA					

CHAPTER 5

NAVIGATING ONLINE DATING

As I said, dating has transformed drastically since my youth. Exchanging phone numbers after meeting someone on a night out was the only way to follow up! Later in the book, I cover different ways to meet potential partners, but I thought I'd explore online dating first. The digital age has brought online dating, apps and social media well and truly into the mix. A good friend of mine who'd taken the plunge to leave a long marriage about six months before I became single, egged me on to join my first dating app. Of course, I had sat next to single friends and enjoyed what seemed like fun swiping right or left, little realising what a challenging experience it could be when you were actually using it.

However I know several success stories (including my daughter who married her second Tinder date). I had also been told that it's rare to meet organically now. There are literally millions of people across the globe now using dating apps, so there's a huge dating pool. The problem is, a lot of the people that use these apps aren't always honest about who they are or what they want. I had watched friends swiping left and right and offered advice from the sidelines. It was my turn now to try and discover that even with those millions of users, it was still very hard to find 'the one'.

As I am no longer working in an office environment or going to events the same way as I did with a corporate career but instead have the solitary life of an author, it definitely limits how you meet new connections. The events I do get to now are 98% women so new tactics and strategy were definitely needed! Online dating had to be tried.

I did discover however, if you let it, online dating can really dent your self-esteem. That's why the work and time spent falling in love with yourself first and being clear what you're looking for and what you won't accept, is a good investment.

As someone who is fundamentally polite, has been taught good manners and is thoughtful of others feelings, the new world of behaviour experienced through online dating was a harsh wake up call.

CREATING THE PERFECT PROFILE

Before you set up your profile, it's worth having spent time preparing. As you are about to launch yourself into the dating world, you want to be sure you are putting your best, beautifully clad foot forward don't you?

The temptation may be to tell a few white lies, use an outdated photo of yourself or leave off information. This can backfire badly. If you aren't honest, how can you expect to make a genuine connection with someone and find a partner who has similar ambitions and goals to you? So if you're going to use sites that require you to build a profile, just make sure you're always truthful about who you are.

I was told by many friends to lie about my age, as 60 is seen as a ceiling to many. "You don't look your age" they insisted, and I was told to beat the parameters set by others, by saying I was younger. I caved in on my first dating app profile, as I was new to it, even though it went against all my principles of being 60 and proud to say my age. After a couple of dates, where I quickly gave my real age, I corrected it and on subsequent apps stayed truthful. In truth it made no difference and I felt SO much better, being my honest and authentic self.

YOUR BIO

So how do you sum yourself up in a few words for your profile? I have had to write work biographies for my CV or for public speaking events, but to sum up my personality and character in a few killer sentences, now that was a bit daunting. To have to showcase my personality, interests, and values in a few paragraphs and pictures. It was like marketing myself, which felt strange and unnatural.

We are taught as children not to show off, but all of a sudden you're being asked to shout out your own praises! In the same way you ditch the inner critic and talk to yourself as your own best friend, I found it helped to think about how others would describe me.

Refer back to the descriptions you filled in on page 12 Now you can use this to support you through this next stage.

Here's a blank template for you to fill in as a starter. Feel free to weave in your personality and sense of humour.

I am _____ , _____ and _____
(3–4 personality traits)

I love to _____ , _____ and _____
(3–4 interests)

I thrive/enjoy _____ , _____ and _____
(lifestyle)

_____ , _____ and _____
are important to me (3 values)

I am looking for _____ , _____ and _____
(3 priorities from your list)

Here's how mine reads;

I'm creative, fun and spontaneous.
I love traveling, cooking, eating and hiking.
I enjoy pushing myself out of my comfort zone with new challenges or adventures and learning from new experiences.

Family, good communication and kindness are important to me.
I am looking for someone to make me laugh, who loves a good conversation and wants to share adventures and experiences with me.
If you make me laugh you can win me over!

THE PHOTOS

I did ask male friends what they would like to see on a dating profile, when it comes to photos and here is their wishlist.

Smiling

Include full length photos

No filters

Solo shots

Use recent photos

PHOTO DO'S

Your photos are not just about how you look, it will give a clear insight into who you are, what you're into and what you're all about.

Men are much more visual than women, and we live in a highly visual world. When a man looks at a picture of a beautiful woman, their brain releases dopamine, often referred to as the "feel-good" neurotransmitter. Dopamine is associated with pleasure, reward, and motivation. It's released in response to pleasurable stimuli, including visual cues of attractiveness.

People are going to be much more picky and have higher expectations about the profile photos they are viewing than they would have done even a few years ago. It makes it quite daunting to think about picking our dating profile pictures. How can we make an impact, stand out from the crowd and reflect our true selves? Listening to expert advice and also getting feedback from male friends, here's what I would recommend.

BE SURE TO CHOOSE GOOD QUALITY PHOTOS

If you choose low quality images, blurry pictures, it will give people the impression that you don't really care, that you don't value yourself or you are hiding something. I remember seeing headless photos thinking why on earth would someone put those photos on unless they were married or in some way embarrassed about the dating experience. Good quality pictures should attract good quality dates, while low quality photos will attract hook-ups. You will only have about five or six photos with which to make a powerful impact so it's worth putting some thought into it.

Put your best photo first as this is what will create the initial attraction (Although most apps have a filter that will put your most/longest viewed photo up front.).

DON'T USE GROUP SHOTS

This is another frustration from people looking at online profiles as they don't know which is you. You need to be the star of the show.

INCLUDE THESE FOUR PHOTOS IF NOTHING ELSE

Shot 1. A smiley headshot

Your headshot has the most work to do out of all your photos as it will be the first one they see. Its main role is to make you look super attractive, warm, approachable and to also ensure you come across as someone people enjoy spending time with. 'Choose smiling over pouting' is the feedback from my male friends. Try to avoid filters, be confident in the unfiltered you as that is who your date will meet.

You need to make this the showstopper that will make you stand out in a sea of faces. Wearing vivid, eye-catching colors, like red, orange or yellow will make you glow or you could choose to have a bold colour in the background.

Shot 2. A recent full body photo

It's essential to include one, up-to-date, full-body photo. One of the most common pieces of feedback I got from men was about women being a different size to their photos in real life. They are wary of being deceived on dating apps, so the relationship is unlikely to go further if a picture is not a real reflection of you. You only need one, and it means if you get a date it's because they are attracted to you as you are. The rest of the photos can focus more on showing off your face and your personality well.

Shot 3. A personality picture

This is your chance to connect with like-minded people through your lifestyle and your personality.

It doesn't have to be complicated. How about a picture of you hugging your dog? Fellow pet lovers will see that, and it will resonate. What men have said they don't want to see though, is just a picture of your pet!

If you're sporty, include a photo of yourself engaged in your favourite activity. Apparently, research suggests that sporty or activity-based photos attract 75% more attention on dating apps than any other photo. I included a gym picture and a hiking photo as being active is such a big part of my life. It could be you're into painting or music festivals. If you are doing something you love in a photo, you will glow and that's very attractive.

Another request from the viewers? Don't use quotes or memes instead of a photo. This does not get your personality across, it's too generic.

This is your opportunity to emphasise the unique, interesting you.

Shot 4. The quirky talking point photo

This is one that will make you stand out, intrigue, surprise or delight people. If nothing else, it's an opportunity for a potential date to find something to comment on. I included in my selection one of me in fancy-dress as Princess Leia! I did have one comment from someone that maybe they could be my Han Solo – so it works!

If you're stuck for ideas, consider what would make you smile?

That's not a huge number of photos to work with, so make sure you're the star of every single one, no group shots, and ensure that each photo says something about you. When choosing my own photos I chose a mixture of full length and face shots.

In fairness, this list should be shared with male friends too, as most men on their profiles seem to have;

Selfies taken from under the chin

Several photos looking the same

Photos in groups with mates and beers

Photos with a fish

Photos on a bike wearing a helmet and cycling glasses

Lying down on a bed, often topless, gazing seductively into camera

All photos with sunglasses

Photos sticking their tongue out (allegedly showing a sense of humour)

No full length photos

Photos of their motorbike

Just torso shots

Sea views / flowers / heart memes

WOO OR BOO?

I soon discovered that the introductory biography across most dating profiles could be anything from a glaringly blank space to a fairly wordy tome, which I found quite fascinating.

I decided that I would only consider potential dates with a biography, as despite being in an environment that was very 'looks' focussed, personality is very important to me. The intro was the first key to unlock my interest.

I found the bio's were incredibly revealing. Some were quite openly misogynistic. A few resonated with bitterness, with gripes about women's profiles as their intro, and some obviously had dating fatigue, with statements such as, "Well I didn't expect to be on here again". None of these filled me with any desire to date these men but it did prompt me to include some red flag warnings on these online characters for you.

ASK THE RIGHT QUESTIONS

So you've essentially swiped right to connect with a total stranger.

Before you start the conversation (and nine times out of ten it will be you who has to start it) go back to all that work in chapter 2 on what's important to you. Dig that back out and think about questions that will unearth whether this potential date can tick any of those boxes.

While you're chatting with a prospective date, it's important to ask leading questions, don't make statements or give the option of a yes or no answer as this is what you will get! An open, leading question means they will answer and that can help you gauge compatibility, understand their values, and get a sense of their personality. A personal lesson I learned was 9 times out of 10, men were generally very lacking in curiosity and rarely asked questions back. The ones who did stood out and, as communication was high on my list of requirements, meant they were a step nearer a date!

THE OPENING LINE

Remember this is the hook to catch their attention!

First impressions are always important, and this is particularly true when it comes to breaking the ice on a dating app. There is so much competition in the online dating space, so a simple "hey" or a waving emoji often won't cut it. These are often unpopular ways to make initial contact as many daters view them as plain lazy. An unoriginal opening line can often be ignored, which can leave you feeling fed up and exhausted by conversations that go nowhere.

The problem is going for a pickup line can feel cheesy, especially if you've experienced some particularly cringy openings online or in real life. You'll recognise the type, everything from "Did it hurt when you fell from heaven" to "I'm no photographer but I can picture us together." While these sorts of lines used to be confined to chatting somebody up in person, they have made their mark in the digital world as daters try the same tactic on somebody they'd like to get to know better. With apps, you don't have the same real-life advantage of flirty smiles and catching somebody's eye first – so there really is a lot riding on that first line. So how do you tread the line between being too bland and too cheesy?

ASK A PERSONALISED QUESTION

If you ask somebody a question about their profile to demonstrate you've paid attention to what they've said rather than just chucking them the same standard opener you've used on everybody else, it shows you've made an effort to craft something original. This can be especially useful if you share the same interests, or you spot something you'd love to know more about. It also lets your date know you've tried rather than mass messaging to see who replies. However, this is tougher if a potential love interest's profile is a bit sparse on detail or you just can't find something you can relate to.

TRY A QUIRKY OPENING LINE

While they might not be for everybody, a jokey or slightly cheesy opening line can be a good way of gauging if somebody shares the same sense of humour as you. If you try a light-hearted opening line and it does not hit the mark, it might be a hint that you and this person might not hit it off anyway. What might seem like a hilarious joke to you may fall flat when you unleash it on somebody else. If you are going down this route, there can be quite a fine art to coming up with a quip that is clever and interest-grabbing with the right amount of humour. You certainly don't want to come on too strong, so it's more about being fun, flirty, and helping to break the tension that can come with chatting with a stranger. Sometimes an interesting and clever question is plenty to show you're trying while giving them something to work with in their response. You can even pose two questions in your opener which gives them the option to answer one if they don't like the other one. You want to demonstrate you are curious to learn more about them while piquing their interest enough to reply.

ASK A QUESTION THAT DEMONSTRATES A SHARED INTEREST

If they have pet photos, they are likely to be an animal lover and will be happy to chat about their beloved pet. Travel photos mean you may be able to relate to somewhere they've been, or have a bit of fun by asking them to describe themselves in a handful of emojis, which allows them to show off their creative side and adds a bit of fun to the chat. You can even be light-hearted about the dating failures you've come up against by asking them the worst opening line they've experienced. Remember, if you're worried about being judged for what you type, people are often just happy that somebody else made the first move.

EVEN IF YOU DO ALL OF THIS, YOU WILL FIND YOU DON'T ALWAYS HEAR BACK

You swiped right on Bumble and after spotting a handsome, eloquent, witty man, you wait for the PING of a match. So then you message him... only to get no response. There's a 24-hour period where responses are allowed and half the time, your match goes away just as quickly as you found him.

So I wondered, if someone looked at your picture, presumably liked what he saw and then swiped right, why weren't they interested enough to write something back?

Here's the potential answers...

1. Being very visual they swiped on a photo but might not have read your profile and when they did, they were no longer interested.

You've sent that first message assuming he liked what he saw. He gets your message, reads your profile and/or looks at the other pictures. He decides, for one reason or another, that he's just not that into you. Women tend to swipe right on those they want to talk to after using all of the information they're given (profile, pictures, etc.). Men, generally, make decisions based on one photo and nothing more.

2. He's not that attracted to you (sorry) and swiped right on everyone.

It's true, some men, knowing how discerning most women are, simply swipe right on everyone to see every single person who likes them in return. So, they may not be interested in 1) dating at all, 2) everyone they swiped on, or 3) even looking at the matches once they come through. This could just be a game of pot luck or an ego boost to them.

3. He forgot.

Sometimes people look at their matches, say they're going to write later, and then simply forget. If someone likes you enough, though, he'll remember to write back... or pay to extend the match. (On Bumble, once a woman writes in her 24-hour period, the man has 24 hours to reply. If one of these conditions is not met, the match goes away.)

4. He's busy.

He has to call his mum for her birthday. He went to the dentist to have a root canal. That report for work is a week overdue! Sometimes people are just busy and dating is not their top priority.

5. His app isn't sending him notifications.

I don't know about you, but I have different notification settings for different apps (I have no interest in my weather app telling me every time there's a little drizzle outside!). Some people don't have their notifications set for the dating apps, the last thing I want in a business meeting is for a Tinder match to chime with a message. It means actively opening the app to check messages. Not everyone does.

6. Your opening message wasn't engaging enough.

Keep your first message short, sweet, and end it with a question. Just remember that anything is better than a "Hi," or "How's your day?" because the only response to these is "Hey" and "good" or "not bad" respectively.

The best way to write a message is to reference something in his profile. So, if he says, "I'm a keen ping pong player," you can say, "Ping pong, huh? I can't say I'm keen like you are, but I bet I could give you a run for your money at tennis. Do you play?"

Sometimes, though, the other person doesn't write a profile that provides any "message bait" (something interesting and unique for you to use in your message), so here are a few examples for when no "message bait" is provided:

- You look like you enjoy being outdoors, right?
- Great sea view. Is that your favourite holiday destination?
- You're a man of mystery! What would you like me to know about you?

7. What do you do if someone you really liked doesn't reply? Do you double message?

Generally, if someone doesn't reply to a message, it indicates that he or she is not interested. But is that true 100% of the time?

Of course not. It's possible they are inundated on the dating app, and there's always a chance that your message got buried in a sea of other messages.

If you do decide to double message, you can say something simple like, "Just wanted to check in since your profile came up again. Hope all is well!" it does not work being accusatory or rude with, "Why did you match with me if you weren't planning to write?" Even if they were inclined to, they won't now. You will never know why some people write back and some don't.

Try not to take the lack of response personally. It's probably not about you. We never know why he replies or doesn't, even if he's expressed interest. Just take it all with a grain of salt, keep swiping and know that the right person for you will reply. You will develop a slightly thicker skin or an ability to smile at the experience the longer it goes on!

So you've got over the first hurdle.

Now the fun part, the foray into a conversation that will help you determine whether they are date material for you.

Here are some examples of questions, but you can adapt to your style or requirements.

A few background facts

- Where did you grow up?
- What line of work are you in?
- What's your favourite thing about your job?
- What are you passionate about?

Their personality and preferences

- How would your friends describe you?
- Are you more of an introvert or extrovert?
- What's your idea of a perfect date?
- Do you prefer a night out or a quiet evening in?

Values and beliefs

- How important is family to you?
- Do you have any personal goals you're working towards?
- What's something you're proud of?

Lifestyle

- Describe your perfect weekend? Asking about their favourite weekend plans gives you an idea of what they like to do which helps judge how compatible you'll be.
- Do you like to travel? What's your favourite destination and what was the best thing about it?

- How would you spend your evenings on a quiet night in?
- Are you a morning person or a night owl?

Interests and hobbies

- What do you like to do in your free time?
- Do you have any hobbies or interests you're really into?
- Are you more of an indoor or outdoor person?
- What's your favourite book, movie, or TV show?

Hopes and dreams

- Where do you see yourself in five years?
- What are some things you still want to achieve in life?
- Do you want to settle down in a particular place, or do you have a dream location?
- How do you feel about long-term relationships?

Fun and light-hearted

- What's something on your bucket list?
- If you could have dinner with any famous person, who would it be?
- What's the most spontaneous thing you've ever done?
- What's a fun fact about you that not many people know?

Deal-breakers and preferences

- What's a deal-breaker for you in a relationship?
- What's the most important quality you're looking for in a partner?
- How do you handle conflicts or disagreements?
- Do you love or hate Marmite?
  (Okay this may not be a deal-breaker)

Relationship and communication style

- How would you describe a healthy relationship?
- How do you prefer to communicate in a relationship?

- What's your love language?
- How do you usually express affection?

These questions can help you have meaningful conversations, allowing you to learn more about each other and determine if there's potential for a deeper connection.

ARE THERE ANY RED FLAGS TO LOOK OUT FOR?

First, not all red flags are the same. Some may simply mean that the person is not ready to date, while others may be indicative of a bigger concern. It's up to you to decide how important each is to you.

Here are some amber/red flags to look out for:

- Photos that are very obviously old. This shows that someone does not have confidence in who he or she is today and is not only living in the past but is trying to deceive you into meeting, using falsely misleading information.

- Too many "lifestyle" photos. What are they trying to prove? Too many (or any) photos with fancy cars, boats, etc. — especially with no one in them — show that this person is trying to compensate for something (looks, personality?) with "stuff." Ultimately, people just want to see who is going to show up on the date. Nothing more, nothing less.

- A long list of things someone does not want in a partner. Whenever I see this, I think, "This person is bitter or not over an ex." Write what you do want, not what you don't. As an addendum to that, anything showing bias towards a whole group of people is a major red flag.

- A long message sharing only information about him or herself and nothing about you. This is a copy/paste job at its finest. Every message should include something specific to you.

- An urgency to connect offline immediately. Where's the fire? If someone says, "Write to me at this email address because my subscription ends tomorrow," then beware.

- A message containing strange links. This one is self-explanatory.

- All "sexy" photos. Either this person is only looking for one thing or is highly self-absorbed. Either one is a turn-off.

- An unwillingness to meet in a timely fashion. In the end, the point of online dating is to meet in person. If someone cannot commit to that, it's time to cut your losses.

- Messages that turn to sex quickly. I have lost count of the times I have been asked what my fantasies are!

NEXT STEP?

I learned the hard way that a phone call or even better a video call done through the app saves a lot of wasted time AND means you don't exchange numbers till you're sure you want to.

- You can see what your match looks like in real life (IRL).

- You can see how the conversation flows.

- You can rule them out if they answer topless
  (Yes, this did happen).

- You can find out if they still live with their mother at 46 (Anyone remember the Ronnie Corbett comedy, 'Sorry?') Yes, this happened too.

- You can see if they are interested and curious about you, after all interested people are interesting.

TERMINOLOGY

A whole new world of acronyms awaited me as I embarked upon online dating, along with new terms for the different behaviours that the anonymity of apps gives.

Ghosting

This dating term refers to the situation when somebody who you've been romantically involved with abruptly cuts all contact without any warning. They end the relationship without explaining why, or even bothering to let you know that they've moved on – leaving you to figure it out on your own after days, weeks and maybe even months of silence.

This is especially difficult in a relationship where you've trusted somebody enough to be intimate with them and the relationship has turned physical. Suddenly, you are ghosted for no reason. It's essentially unfinished business that leaves you feeling confused, abandoned and questioning what you did wrong to be dropped so abruptly. Ironically, despite how you are feeling, the real issue is with the person who does the ghosting, and it's worth remembering that it is their problem not yours, as you are not the one to blame.

Zombieing

This is where you've been left hanging by a ghost and then just as you are starting to get over them, they come back with lots of promises and poor excuses for their disposable manners and behaviour – only to prime you up, to be ghosted again!

Be under no false illusions, once somebody has ghosted you, they will know they can get away with it if you allow them back into your life to do it again. It may sound harsh but it's true. It can particularly add insult to injury if you've already been hurt in the past by the person who ghosted you. Be kind to yourself and remember to set and maintain strong boundaries of how you want to be treated, at the first sign of this behaviour don't chase them. Instead put your phone down – or even better, block them and move on.

Breadcrumbing

This is, in a nutshell, leading somebody on. It's when somebody that you're dating drops subtle hints of wanting a relationship with you but then they come and go as they please or are just plain inconsistent. You never know where you really stand or what the intentions are of the person doing this to you.

Their behaviour often leaves you feeling confused, and it can be quite an emotional rollercoaster because you love it when they get in touch and really enjoy the time you spend together. That rush of adrenaline when you see each other may feel great, but the rollercoaster ride you've taken is ultimately very damaging as they give you just enough hope that they may commit with no intention or action that they ever will.

Lack of clarity in dating is hugely detrimental for your self-esteem and can lead to longer term anxiety when it comes to meeting people which can ultimately sabotage your dating journey. If you've fallen victim to any of these toxic behaviours, you can start to mistrust your judgement and become fearful of the good people that you encounter along the way who are much better suited to you.

Catfishing

Catfishing means someone is using a fake identity to trick you. It could just be using fake photos, doctored photos or very old photos to lure you into a chat or a date when they don't look like their profile. Or at worst, they are trying to trick you into believing you're in a real online friendship or romance with them. Once you trust the catfish, they may: embarrass, humiliate or upset you by sharing your secrets online or revealing to others that you fell for their trick. The internet is a world of endless possibilities and the people hiding behind their screens aren't always who they say they are. Catfishing has become a very common tactic on dating platforms.

Catfish can be cyber criminals who use fake photos and names while messaging you in a very believable way, to gain your trust and find out your personal information. It's important to be aware of the threats related to catfish on dating platforms and learn how to protect yourself from them.

A romance scam starts as a catfisher building a fake relationship with their target to steal their money and personal information. Catfishers invest time into their relationship with their targets (weeks, months, years) to create believable, detailed stories on why they need money. These cyber criminals can be very convincing, with tales about needing money for urgent healthcare or important business-related expenses. Romance scams are the second most common cause of financial fraud in Canada. Understand the risks and stay aware by learning what signs to look out for.

How do you recognise a catfish? It can be difficult to see a cyber criminal for who they are when you have an affection or relationship with them. Here are some of the most common signs of a catfisher:

- the person expresses their love for you without ever having met you in person

- the person always has excuses for not making a video call or just doesn't show their face for various reasons

- the person tries to isolate you from people who have doubts about your virtual relationship

Catfishers will try to make their fake identity seem as realistic and interesting as possible. If something seems too good to be true, it likely is.

Catfish profiles often use photos of real people. Do some research, like searching their profile name on a search engine and seeing if what appears matches what they have presented to you. If the profile has no other accounts with the same name, it is likely a catfish. If the person does have other accounts, look into details, like their friendships and the engagement on their photos.

Here are some signs to be aware of from a catfisher's profile:

- their account was created recently

- they don't have many posts

- their number of friends is quite low

- they have connections with profiles all over the world and don't seem to interact with them

There are many signs to identify a catfish, but some are more apparent than others. If you are still unsure if your connection is a catfish, ask them specific questions to learn more about them, like their place of birth, place of work, residence and parents' names.

Some profiles can seem too good to be true, trust your intuition.

ONS
Not the Office for National Statistics, this is One Night Stand.

ENM
Ethical Non-Monogamy means being in romantic or sexual relationships with multiple partners at the same time, with the knowledge and consent of everyone involved.

Partners can decide if they want their relationship to be committed, casual, long-term, short-term, romantic, sexual, or any combination of these things. They mutually agree on what types of connections they'll pursue and not pursue, both with each other and with other people, and they can set any parameters or expectations they'd like to make all parties feel comfortable.

NSA

No Strings Attached – don't go looking here if you want a serious relationship.

Non-vanilla

If a vanilla relationship = traditional, then anyone who describes themselves as non-vanilla is looking for something out of the ordinary, whether kinky, non-monogamous, swinging, bondage... if you are curious and into this the only way to find out what type of out of the ordinary it may be, is to ask for more details!

Sexy positivity

I found it intriguing that when faced with having to only pick 5 words to describe their interests, that this came up on so many men's profiles as one of them. I'm sure most women looking for a partner would be looking for something more revealing about them? In having a few dates, it seemed a lot of relationships had ended with their sex life or intimacy having dried up and that they felt the need to make sure their next relationship entailed having sex! Hence this specific choice.

FLR .

Female led relationship (more to follow in Chapter 7).

CHAPTER 6

THE MATCHMAKERS TOP TIPS

I am very lucky to have as a close friend, Michelle Begy, founder of Ignite Dating who has given me some great advice and here are some of her top tips that helped me as I navigated this whole new world of dating.

HOW DO I HANDLE REJECTION?

After coming out of a long-term marriage or relationship, putting yourself out there does make you feel vulnerable. You've spent time finding the right words for your dating profile, spent hours searching the apps or trying new experiences to meet someone, balancing everything else going on in your life, which can all take the shine out of the journey over time. So one of the most difficult elements when starting dating again, comes when being faced with rejection. While it can be disheartening, understanding how to handle rejection with grace and resilience is essential. Michelle's tips to help me manage rejection, protect my self-esteem and dust myself off to continue this dating journey with confidence – even when faced with a no thank you.

Understanding rejection

Rejection is an inevitable part of dating. Whether it's after a first date, during the initial stages of getting to know someone, or even further down the line, it's important to recognise that rejection is not a reflection of your worth. Instead, it's a natural part of finding a compatible partner. They aren't rejecting you as a person, they are rejecting words on a screen, they don't know the real, fantastic you.

Rejection happens to everyone. Even the most successful daters will have experienced that disheartened feeling somewhere along their journey before they met the one. It's important to remember that it's not always about you; sometimes it's the other person's circumstances. Mindset or preferences play a significant role in them choosing not to move forward with you. Just as you have a criterion that you would like a potential partner to meet, so do they and unfortunately, they don't always align.

That said, every rejection brings you one step closer to finding the right person for you. Every date or conversation is a learning curve. It allows you to reflect on what is important to you in a partner and often allows you to open yourself up to possibilities that you may have never considered. As matchmakers we constantly come up against rejections based on age or height for example, but when they actually get to know each other and see more of the person in front of them beyond the age or height that they were set on, it is quite often one of the first things that then changes. So, while rejection can be disappointing, think of it as a redirection towards the person you're supposed to be with.

Coping with rejection

While rejection can be disappointing and heartbreaking, particularly if you were growing fond of the other person, when faced with rejection, it's crucial to manage it in a healthy way. The first step is to acknowledge your feelings. It's perfectly okay to feel upset, disappointed, or even angry about the situation. Acknowledge these emotions, talk them through with your matchmaker or a trusted friend, but don't dwell on them. Allow yourself to process the rejection before moving forward with your dating journey, to ensure that you're not taking any negative feelings into your next potential relationship.

Remember that every rejection is a redirection. The person who rejected you simply wasn't the right fit, and that's okay. Stay positive and open-minded about future possibilities as even in the most successful relationships, both parties had to kiss a few frogs before they found their prince or princess.

While often easier said than done, avoid overthinking. Over analysing the situation can lead to unnecessary self-doubt. As mentioned before, it may not be about you but by dissecting and internalising the situation you may be chipping away at your self-esteem and confidence over something that has nothing to do with who you are. Instead of obsessing over what went wrong, focus on what you can learn from the experience.

Rejection can be a valuable learning experience. Instead of viewing it as a failure, use it as an opportunity for growth and reflect on the interaction. Consider whether there were any red flags or areas where communication could have been improved. This reflection isn't about self-criticism but about understanding how to approach dates more effectively. This is where working with a matchmaker can really help, as they have an outside perspective and are able to mediate between both sides, asking for feedback, to work out what happened and how you can learn and move on from the experience in a healthy way.

Use the time when dating to work on personal growth and self-improvement. Whether it's improving your communications skills, trying new hobbies, or focusing on your well-being, investing in yourself will now only boost your confidence but will make you more attractive to future partners.

Maintaining confidence while moving forward

After dealing with rejection, it's important to keep your confidence intact. In those moments where you feel disheartened and disappointed with your dating journey, spend time with friends and loved ones who uplift and support you. Their encouragement can help you stay positive and motivated and remind you of all the fabulous traits that make you who you are.

Remember that dating is a journey, not a destination. Keep dating and rejection in perspective, as it is only one aspect of the journey. Stay focused on the bigger picture and the potential for finding a meaningful connection.

Don't forget, there are also people out there who are qualified to help. If you're finding it difficult to navigate the dating world on your own, consider enlisting the help of a matchmaker. A professional can provide personalised advice and support, helping you find the right partner more efficiently.

There's no denying that handling rejection in the dating world requires resilience, self-awareness, and a positive mindset. By understanding that rejection is a natural part of the dating process, learning from each experience, and staying confident, you'll be better equipped to continue your journey with optimism. Remember, every rejection brings you closer to finding the right match. Stay true to yourself, keep an open heart, and trust that the right person is out there, waiting to meet you.

HOW DO I END A CONNECTION POLITELY?

Michelle shared the best advice on how to deal with rejection after you are turned down by somebody in the dating world. After a long time in a relationship, this was new to me. However, what was equally new was how to deal with what happens when you are the one who isn't feeling it. As a kind person, it can be hard to be the cause of somebody else's disappointment, and I know I worried over how somebody would react to being turned down.

Michelle counselled me, that uncomfortable as you may feel with telling somebody you're not interested, it does pay to be upfront and honest about your feelings. It's unfair and may lead to further disappointment down the line if you give somebody you've been dating false hope. One of my non-negotiables was not to accept someone who plays games, and most people react well to an honest answer about how you feel, even if you feel you need to soften the blow.

I was not alone in dreading rejecting somebody, it feels uncomfortable and awkward. It's tricky to find the correct words and of course, you worry they will take the rejection extremely personally and with hurt feelings. However, I learned it's important to remember you're letting them know that you don't think you'd be compatible, rather than criticising who they are. Done in the right way, a rejection will hopefully not be taken too personally.

Here's Michelle's top tips for effectively handling a rejection so you can both feel the situation was handled well and you both feel empowered. Whether you've only exchanged a few messages or you've been on a few dates, find out more about how to handle rejection the right way.

Try and avoid ambiguity

Your heart might be in the right place but beating around the bush can cause confusion and string things out. However, you don't need to be harsh to be direct. You can always pair the rejection with a compliment or a polite sentence or two about how you enjoyed getting to know them. The idea is being clear that whilst you felt some connection, after all you shared time and energy with them, it is not strong enough for you to dive in and you don't want to pursue the match any further. Being unclear in your response can cause confusion as the other person will receive mixed signals and think you are still potentially interested. Using wishy-washy excuses could send signals that you'll be interested in the future.

You don't need to apologise

Saying sorry implies you've done something wrong but you haven't. There is no need to say sorry for not being interested in somebody. You can explain you are flattered by their attention but be clear that you don't want to take things any further.

Text messages are OK in the early days

If you have been chatting to somebody casually or you've only had a date or two, it's fine to send a message saying you don't want to pursue a romantic relationship. However, if you've been seeing somebody for months or have been intimate with them then they deserve more than a text that says it's over. This should preferably be done face to face or via a video call.

Never ghost somebody

Even if you don't want to let somebody down, it never pays to ghost them. Ghosting is hurtful and leads to a lack of closure, as the other person doesn't understand the reason you disappeared off the face of the earth. They may also blame themselves for things coming to an abrupt halt. The only time it's OK to ghost somebody is if they react negatively to your rejection and become angry or hurtful.

It's always important to remember there is a human being behind every dating profile and it can be unfair to treat people in a way you would not like to be treated. Even if you don't see any potential in the pairing, make sure you are being clear, honest, and upfront. That way they can move on to the next person, who may well turn out to be perfect for them.

WHAT IF THERE'S NO CHEMISTRY ON YOUR FIRST DATE?

Are you quick to write somebody off after a first date that didn't lead to an instant connection? I was.

You can feel dejected if an initial date did not spark instant chemistry. You can see it as a sign that it's not worth pursuing another meet-up with this person, especially if the first date was decidedly mediocre, because they feel it won't lead anywhere.

Of course, if the first date was excruciatingly bad, it's clear that you won't be spending any more time together. However, there are many good reasons to give it another shot if somebody has potential, but the first date just didn't set the world on fire.

Firstly, it's worth considering how nerve-wracking first dates can be. There can be a lot of pressure on that first meeting, and being nervous means people won't relax and be themselves. Nerves can make that first encounter awkward, which is why some don't follow up with a second date. However, the person you meet might be having a tough week or they just struggle to make an easy-going, relaxed first impression.

While an instant spark can happen, it certainly should not be expected. When you have that instant fireworks when you meet someone, this is lust based, which isn't the foundation for a long-term relationship. What usually happens is that the relationship moves quickly to an intimacy, without establishing if you have the same values or future aspirations, only to burn out a couple of weeks down the line.

Many great relationships start with a slow burn, and it can certainly take more than one date to build a connection. The key question you need to ask is whether you think there is enough there to make it worth seeing this person again. A lot of experts agree that, unless you encounter major red flags, you should give it two more dates to see if there's enough there for you to consider a future together.

Here are Michelle's top tips for deciding whether it's worth investing more time to see if you have a true connection.

Remember, a second date can be a lot more relaxed:

The first time you meet you are essentially strangers. With the second date, you can naturally be a lot more authentic as you relax and just concentrate on getting to know each other better. If your first date was grabbing a quick coffee, then consider an activity-based date to further break the ice and see how the person acts in a different situation. First dates can end up feeling like job interviews, with all the questions flying back and forward, so it does pay to try again to get a better idea of what somebody is really like. With a second date you can really show your true personality and feel a lot more like yourself.

Think about what you enjoyed about the first meeting:

While there might not have been an instant attraction, consider what you did like about the time you spent with this person. Did you have fun? Did they make you laugh? Was the conversation interesting? Then you have good foundations for seeing them again.

Remember, instant chemistry is not necessarily a good thing:

Rapid-fire romance does not necessarily translate into a happy relationship. The love-at-first-sight feeling often isn't sustainable, rarely happens later in life in the long run as you can overlook those all-important characteristics of a person when you are blindsided by your initial physical attraction to them.

Make sure your date is respectful:

Did they show up on time, listen properly and ask you questions? Or did they talk non-stop about themselves and were rude to the waiting staff? It can sometimes be clear who is and isn't worth investing more time in.

More time can help you assess signs of compatibility:

Great relationships are often built on shared values, interests and lifestyle aspirations. The more you get to know somebody, the more likely it is you'll grow to like them based on what you learn about them. If there are signs you may have a good chance of compatibility, then it might well be worth pursuing things further.

While attraction might not be there from the outset, you may well like the person enough to consider meeting again. Having a couple more dates should give you a much clearer picture of whether your values align and whether a connection may grow. You might just remain friends or go your separate ways, but, without any obvious deal-breakers it can be worthwhile to invest more time in a person who may turn out to be perfect for you.

HELP, I HAVE 'DATING BURNOUT', WHAT DO I DO?

Whilst it seemed like fun looking at it from the outside, online dating was much tougher than I had expected. There's no doubt that these days we are all extremely busy people. If your phone isn't constantly pinging with messages and emails, it's probably out of battery. From the latest news on your family WhatsApp group and appointment reminders from your local hairdresser, to work emails and updates from your dog walker, there's a lot to take in on a daily basis.

If you add an online app-based approach to dating into the mix, well, life can get even more frantic. Online dating apps are designed to make it easy to connect quickly with lots of people at the swipe of a screen. While this may seem like a benefit if you're looking to meet somebody new, it turns out it's quite stress-inducing if you get too swept up in it all. There is the temptation to think that the person of your dreams is there, somewhere, buried in those countless online profiles, so all you need to do is keep up the momentum – and the swiping – to find them. But a quick five-minute search can turn into hours assessing person after person. Suddenly that relaxed night on the sofa, with a well-earned glass of wine after a long week, turns from a chilled box set marathon to your hands creeping to the phone for just a quick look. Before you know it, it's the early hours.

If a search for love is starting to feel quite labour intensive and you're getting increasingly exhausted with it all, it can be a sign that you are 'panic dating' and at risk of dating burnout. But it's not just having so much choice at your fingertips that can lead to getting carried away – the temptation to 'panic date' can come from an array of different sources.

Perhaps it's a reluctance to say no to a date if you're invited on one. A lot of singletons can feel the pressure to be out there constantly and worry that by pressing pause on their dating journey for even a short while, it can mean they'll miss out. If you're constantly focusing on the next date, or rushing to another meeting that very same evening, be sure this approach works for you as it's easy to feel burned out if you're already juggling a hectic schedule. It's tempting to agree to numerous dates on your quest to find the perfect partner but remember – dating is meant to be fun. If it's starting to feel like a chore, or you've got zero motivation to get out there, it's a sign you need to reassess your approach to dating.

You may also be feeling subtle pressure from your friendship group to get coupled up, especially if a steady stream of engagement announcements and wedding invites are coming your way. It can be hard when your single friends dwindle, especially if you are finding it hard to feel 100% content with the freedom of singledom.

You may even be toying with the temptation to think about rekindling with an ex. This may come as a result of feeling like everybody else is coupling up, but if there were good reasons behind the decision to call it a day, it's probably not a good idea to try and pick up where you left off. They are usually an ex for a reason!

If all this sounds familiar, then don't despair. There are a few simple tricks and techniques to solve a frantic approach to dating.

Take a step back

Firstly, contrary to popular belief it can be helpful to take a step away from dating and take some time for yourself, providing plenty of time for reflection about what's not working and the changes you need to make. Self-care is important to ensure you're looking after number one, and taking a break for even a short while can mean you return to dating feeling energised and confident. It'll also provide some valuable balance and help you focus on other parts of your life that make you happy.

Refocus on self-love

A break from dating can be the perfect time to concentrate on what you really want from a partner and a relationship. Try not to sweat how long the break is – you won't be missing out if you really invest the time in ensuring dating is fun again once you're really ready to get back out there. You can then return to a more purposeful dating journey, being more selective with the time you dedicate to dating, focusing more on who you meet and the types of dates you'll really enjoy.

Trust your instincts

Don't waste time on a date if you've got a gut feeling they're not right for you – there's plenty more fish in the sea and you'll have a lot more fun if you see the romance potential shining through their profile.

Turn off notifications

One thing I find helps with online dating is turning the alerts off the apps (or even better don't have it on your phone) and having a specific, dedicated time to swipe. That way, you are in control of the apps, rather than them controlling you. It can also help to stop dating burnout occurring.

So, if you're getting the feeling your dating journey is not quite working for you at the moment, remember it can pay to take a step back and have a good look at what you really want. And when you're ready to date again, it'll be all the more fun and enjoyable!

DATING A MULTI DATER?

So in the early stages of online dating, it is important to realise that your date, like you, may be exploring being single for the first time in a long while. That said, it's still an odd feeling sensing the person you are chatting to on a dating app is busy juggling multiple conversations with other people. You may find they drag their feet replying to your messages and come across as extremely busy when you suggest meeting up.

Michelle's advice on this is that in the dating world it's certainly not unusual to encounter somebody who is dating multiple people at once. Some singletons prefer not to keep their eggs all in one basket, especially in the early days of dating where they are investing time in getting to know several people simultaneously. However, dating more than one person at a time can get messy, especially when feelings develop.

For many it makes sense to get to know several people at once, as it takes a lot of time to move from the initial chats to meeting in person. If you realise you are not compatible after a couple of dates, you've got to start all over again searching for somebody new. When you meet online you've got no idea what the outcome is going to be, so for some it makes sense to be connecting with several people to widen the pool of people that might be right for you. It's known as roster dating, a strategy where you casually see more than one romantic interest at a time, and people eventually melt away as you invest more time into solidifying a connection with the person you are most interested in.

As well as finding out who you share a spark with, meeting a range of people helps you understand your own needs and figure out what you want out of a relationship. With each date you get a better knowledge of the sort of person you gel with and what you don't like. It can be a lot of fun to meet new people and keep things casual without having to consider everything that comes with a committed relationship.

Of course, there are drawbacks to this sort of dating. It can take a lot of time and energy to commit to multiple chats and dates, which could lead to dating burnout if you're not careful. It can be difficult enough to make time for dating one person, let alone several. It can be very embarrassing to forget things dates have told you, or get details about their lives wrong, purely because you're juggling meet-ups with too many people at once. When you are burnt out by the whole process of dating, then you can easily become overwhelmed and dating 'anybody and everybody', just seems like a chore.

Dating somebody who is seeing multiple people

You may be keen on only pursuing one love interest at a time, so where does that leave you if the person you are dating is seeing multiple people? Problems can develop when you get more attached, and you may start to feel jealous and resent the fact they're still dating. Their casual approach may suggest they aren't looking for a relationship so you can end up getting hurt if you are hoping they will become exclusive in the end. You may have not even been on the same page about what's going on, as the person you're seeing might expect you are also dating multiple people. It may take time until it emerges that they are dating other people, and you may be upset when you realise you are not the only person they've been seeing.

It's worth being honest about your feelings about wanting to be exclusive and then see what their reaction is. If they say they don't want to commit and prefer to be dating non-exclusively, then you need to decide if this is an arrangement you can tolerate being involved in. If the answer is no, then it's time to walk away.

In those early days of dating, it's important to manage your expectations and not get too carried away until things have had a chance to develop. As much as you might be tempted to, asking somebody if they would consider being exclusive after only a couple of dates might risk scaring them off. There's always a risk that if you decide to date non-exclusively, people you are meeting might want to cut ties as they prefer to have your undivided attention.

When it comes to dating, you need to decide what works for you. Trust your gut feeling and if you prefer to date exclusively, then avoid getting involved with anybody who isn't in the same place as you. Communicate clearly to them that you are seeking a monogamous relationship and if they aren't, then your core values don't align. Consider working with a matchmaker if you'd like a helping hand on your dating journey, because teaming up with the experts means you can sit back and relax while we find you amazing people to meet.

HOW DO I END A BAD DATE?

In a perfect world every date you went on would be full of interesting conversation and fascinating insights into the other person's life. Even if your date doesn't set your world on fire, the evening would be fun, satisfying and a good use of your precious spare time.

However, unfortunately not all dates end up like this. First meetings don't always go well, leaving people desperate to pull any excuse out of the bag to be able to leave what might be an excruciatingly dull evening. According to recent research from Britannia Rescue, daters will only tolerate 51 minutes of a bad date before making an excuse to leave. More than a fifth of those surveyed say they've left a bad date halfway through, with daters taking an average of 25 minutes to decide if they and their date have a spark.

Why bad dates happen

It's not unusual to end up on a bad date. You can only glean so much from an online dating profile so meeting in real life is really the first opportunity to suss out what somebody is really like. Some daters find several pre-screening phone calls/video calls are helpful to judge whether somebody is on the same page as them and worth getting to know better. Sometimes though, whatever vetting process you've tried out, a face-to-face meet-up is what it takes to reveal there is zero chemistry between you both and you just don't click, even as friends. Things can also go awry when your date's behaviour is off-putting, or they don't match up to what they've told you about in their profile. The conversation may be falling flat, and the long pauses aren't romantic ones. Sometimes, unfortunately, there's something about this person that leaves you feeling unsafe, which means it is certainly the right thing to do to call time on the date immediately.

So, things aren't going as expected and you're keen not to dedicate any more time to something which you see has zero potential. How do you make an exit that won't offend your date and risk hurting their feelings?

Here are some tips.

Make it short

A micro-date can be a good idea for a first meeting, to see if there is enough between you to warrant a proper first date. It's a good idea to meet for coffee or a casual drink, which gives you an easy out if things aren't going well. There's nothing worse than being committed to a set menu or an activity you can't get out of with somebody you really aren't gelling with. You can also have something else lined up to add a time constraint to your meeting, and they won't feel dumped if they knew in advance that you were meeting friends later that night. Try choosing venues where if the date is going well, you can extend it. I found that a nice bar for drinks was good if you then could add small plates if it was going well.

Be honest

It's natural to not enjoy confrontation and want to protect somebody's feelings, but it can be the kindest way to be upfront about the fact you're not feeling it. It is worth being honest that you did not feel a romantic connection, while expressing gratitude for them coming out to meet you. It's about letting them know it's not working out the way you hoped without giving false hope that you'll see them again in the future. Try not to fall back on lines like "I'll text you" or "let's do this again" when you have absolutely no intention of doing so.

If you are not feeling safe

It's best to meet in public, where you can seek out the help of bar or restaurant staff to help call you a taxi if you are concerned about how a date is behaving, or simply call a friend to come and collect you.

Don't put up with bad behaviour

If somebody is being rude or offensive, don't feel bad about paying your share of the bill and leaving – you don't owe them an excuse.

When to give somebody the benefit of the doubt

It can pay to be open-minded, as sometimes nerves can easily sabotage the first part of your date. If you see romance potential in this person, and it does appear they are trying, it can be worth sticking around to see how things progress. Every date is a learning experience so by trying to establish a connection with this person, you'll not be completely wasting your time.

Lying is never a great idea in the dating world, as it can spiral and lead to all sorts of complicated stories being fabricated. Sometimes it pays to have in mind a reason you might need to bail early, such as your early meeting in the morning, or wanting to ensure you don't miss the last train. Having a pre-prepared excuse which is true means you don't have to resort to faked emergency calls from friends, or even worse, going to the bathroom and never returning!

CHAPTER 7

THE CHARACTERS THAT CAME OUT OF THE WOODWORK

Of course I matched with some nice, sorted, dateable men. I went on some great dates, made some new friends, enjoyed a couple of short romances, as well as meeting people who were nice enough, but with whom I had no spark.

But there certainly were some interesting characters that tried to match with me and whom I avoided. Here's my guide on what to watch out for including a tongue in cheek bio, but I will share before I go into detail some of the oddest lines men put in their opening gambit.

- *I am abnormally attracted to small breasts.*

- *All I am looking for is a fun, busty bird, is that too much to ask?*

- *I am hoping you're over 45 and like wearing tights.*

- *I play CoD, watch Sci-Fi and sometimes I 'Beat Sabre.'*

- *If you wear heels you're a keeper.*

- *Is there any fit, not fat ladies left? Not into out of shape weirdos with tits.*

- *I guarantee you at least 3 orgasms a week.*

THE COUGAR HUNTER

BIO

Name: *Young Buck (Because "Toy Boy" is too overused)*

Age: *28 – but I have put 45 so I can match with you :)*

About Me: *I'm here for the mature, the marvellous, and the mojitos. I believe life starts at 40, yours, not mine. I am looking for that confidence in ALL matters that comes with age (and hopefully a bit of flexibility if you take your cod liver oil). Let's skip the small talk and head straight to the part where you teach me life lessons and I remind you how to use TikTok.*

What I experienced

I want to be clear that I have no issues with a woman dating a younger man, in fact I get frustrated by the inconsistencies of media reporting, that always comment on a woman dating a man 20 years her junior, when the reverse would go unnoticed. I found it really irritating that even if the men matching with me were only a few years younger, I'd be asked how I feel about dating a younger man! I'm sure that never happens the other way around. I did date men in their early 40's, and it was never about the age for me, it was always about the person. For me what I noticed was a difference in vitality and enthusiasm for life that many older men had lost.

What I wasn't expecting on the apps, was the number of young men in their mid-twenties who put their ages as late forties in order that the algorithm paired them with older women.

This must have happened close to 10 times. I personally had an issue with dating someone younger than my son, but I would not judge another woman doing so if that was her choice.

Okay, the photos should have given them away, but were often a bit blurry and with so much use of filters, it wasn't always obvious until the chat started.

They would either quickly confess, or my gut instinct would prompt me to ask a direct question on age.

So what is the appeal of the older woman?

Turns out quite a few things!

Older women often have more life experience, which can be attractive to younger men who are looking for someone who knows what they want and has a clearer sense of self. We tend to be more emotionally stable and mature, which can create a sense of security and comfort in the relationship. We, as older women are often perceived to be less interested in games or drama, with direct, bold, straightforward communication, which can be attractive and seductive to younger men.

We are often more confident in ourselves and understand our desires, which can be appealing, and educational, to younger men who might be drawn to that confidence. If they believe older women have more sexual experience, it can be intriguing for younger men who are interested in exploring their sexuality with a knowledgeable partner who is not afraid to say what they like and instruct! Sometimes it may not just be sexual confidence and experience that's attractive, they might be looking for a partner who can offer guidance or mentorship in various aspects of life, from career advice to personal growth.

Relationships with older women can sometimes carry less pressure in terms of long-term commitments or the expectation to start a family, allowing for a more relaxed dynamic. Many older women are financially and emotionally independent, which can be attractive to men who appreciate a partner with their own established life. I never came across anyone looking for a sugar mummy but I'm sure there are some out there.

In a couple of approaches, dating an older woman was clearly a buzz for some men, with the idea that everyone would look as you walked into a room together, as if you were breaking society's norms, which seemed to be exciting and different.

Some younger men might simply be curious about what it's like to date someone older and are exploring different types of relationships to see what suits them best.

Some men are simply more attracted to older women physically and emotionally, preferring their company to that of women their own age. It turned out in my conversations, that many had had an experience with an older woman at a fairly young age which had left them with a permanent penchant for a more mature partner.

Although it still seems controversial or gossip worthy, relationships between younger men and older women can be based on genuine connections and mutual respect, just like any other relationship. There are many great examples in the public eye, Joan Collins and Percy Gibson, Sam and Aaron Taylor-Johnson and Heidi Klum and Tom Kaulitz proving age is no barrier to long lasting love.

Films such as Bridget Jones, Mad about the Boy and Baby Girl, both cover (albeit very different) relationships of an older woman and younger man.

THE DOM DESIRER

BIO

Name: *Whatever You Want It To Be*

Age: *45 (but I can role-play any age if that's your thing)*

About Me: *Just a shy, compliant soul looking for someone to call the shots. Your wish is my command—literally. I'm here to fulfil your dreams, as long as they include bossing me about and picking tonight's takeaway. Swipe right, and I'll even let you pick my profile picture.*

What I experienced

Maybe I give off a boss woman vibe, or maybe many older women will experience the same approach from a certain genre of men, but it didn't take long before I was asked how I felt about a Female Led relationship (which I actually had to Google). When I asked out of curiosity what it was they wanted, it went from someone who wanted looking after financially, to someone who wanted to be dominated in the bedroom.

So what is the appeal of an FLR?

When a man asks for a Female-Led Relationship (FLR), he is expressing a desire to be in a relationship where the woman takes the dominant or leading role in various aspects of the partnership. The dynamic can apparently vary widely from Light to Full FLR. FLRs can vary in intensity. Some may be "light," where the woman leads in certain areas, while others may be more "full" FLRs, where the woman has comprehensive control over many or all aspects of the relationship. Every FLR is unique, and the level of control and leadership can be tailored to fit the desires of both partners depending on the preferences of the individual.

In an FLR, the woman is generally the one who makes most or all of the important decisions within the relationship, such as financial matters, household management, and social activities. The man is ideally looking to their partner for guidance and direction, valuing her judgment and leadership in the relationship.

They may want a reversal of traditional gender roles, where the man may take on responsibilities that are traditionally seen as feminine, such as homemaking or caregiving, while the woman takes on traditionally masculine roles, such as being the primary breadwinner or making major decisions.

FLR may involve a consensual power exchange, where the man willingly submits to the woman's authority. This can be in everyday decisions or more formalized aspects of the relationship. The dynamic focuses on empowering the woman to lead, often celebrating her strength, independence and authority.

With regard to the sexual dynamics in some FLRs, the woman may take on a sexually dominant role, setting the terms of sexual activity and establishing boundaries. This can be a key aspect of the relationship for some couples. The man may derive satisfaction from being in a more submissive role, enjoying the control and authority that the woman exercises. For some, an FLR might include elements of kink or BDSM, where the power dynamic extends into their sexual relationship.

An FLR is typically based on mutual consent and clear communication. Both partners must be comfortable with the dynamic, and there should be ongoing discussions about boundaries, expectations and desires making it a highly customizable relationship model. Despite the power dynamics, an FLR can be a very supportive and loving relationship, where both partners work together to ensure each other's happiness and well-being.

Whilst this is not a society norm, it can be empowering for women while offering men a chance to explore a different type of relationship dynamic.

THE FLASHER

BIO

Name: *Big Bob*

Age: *49 (but you won't be looking at my face)*

About Me: *Why waste time with pleasantries when I can just show you the goods? I'm direct, confident, and always ready to send more (just say the word). I believe in transparency, though I hear it's not always appreciated. Fun fact: I don't even own trousers—life's too short for unnecessary layers. Swipe right for an inbox surprise.*

What I experienced

I had obviously heard about women being sent unsolicited pictures of men's genitals or let's just get down to basics and call them "dick pics" on dating apps. Sending unsolicited explicit images is inappropriate and can be distressing or violating.

I misguidedly thought they may be as a result of the recipient having encouraged them or that they were sent after a long time conversing, and had gotten to a point in the conversation where it was not going to be a shock. But no. I learned quite quickly in 2–3 instances that there are some men out there who it seems were just dying to flash their wares!

The line before they did? I am 'blessed' in that department.

So why do men want to send uncensored pictures?

It seems it's a result of a whole combination of factors, including misconceptions, misguided expectations, and psychological motivations.

Men tend to be stimulated visually, women verbally. Look at the success of The Fifty Shades of Grey novels! Some men mistakenly believe that women will be as visually stimulated by explicit images as they are, assuming that sending a picture will generate excitement. This misunderstanding stems from an acute lack of awareness of how women are stimulated.

With easy access to pornography, where women often appear to be aroused by male genitals, it can lead men to falsely believe that this will translate to real-life interactions, that you're ready to be the leading lady.

Sending explicit images can sometimes be a way for men to seek validation or an ego boost. They may hope for positive feedback or compliments, which can affirm their attractiveness or masculinity. In some cases, men who are insecure about their appearance or desirability might send these pictures in an attempt to receive reassurance.

The relative anonymity provided by dating apps can lead to a lack of inhibition, where men feel emboldened to behave in ways they wouldn't in face-to-face interactions. I did often point out, would they do this in a bar to someone they just started talking to? The perceived lack of consequences might encourage riskier behaviour. The ease of creating and using relatively anonymous dating profiles means men can behave inappropriately without facing significant repercussions.

Some men might see sending such pictures as a low-risk way to quickly escalate a conversation to a sexual level, testing your boundaries, especially if they think there's a chance of reciprocation. Some men use these pictures as a way to test how receptive the other person is to sexual content.

For some men, sending explicit pictures might be linked to voyeuristic or exhibitionist tendencies, where they derive sexual pleasure from exposing themselves to others.

In some cases, men might misinterpret a conversation as being more sexually charged than it actually is, leading them to believe that an explicit image would be welcome or appropriate. Flirting on text does not have the nuances of body language to help navigate responses.

Each to their own, but I didn't go on any dates with men who sent me a full frontal as part of their chat up approach, instead blocking them.

THE NARCISSIST

BIO

Name: *Mr Right (Literally)*

Age: *54 The perfect age*

About Me: *Stop searching—you've found perfection. My hobbies include admiring myself, waiting for compliments, and photoshopping my Instagram pics. I'm looking for someone who can handle being the second most important person in the relationship. Must be fluent in ego-stroking.*

What I experienced

I definitely found myself dating a couple of men with narcissistic tendencies. I wish I had known what to look out for, or tips on how to manage them. After starting with love bombing to win me over, they then switched to swings in behavior, creating dramas that meant I felt on the back foot.

Why should you avoid a narcissist?

Spotting a narcissist on a dating app can be tricky because they often present themselves as charming and confident. However, there are certain signs you can look out for to help identify potential narcissistic traits:

Their profile may be filled with achievements, awards, and glamorous photos. They often emphasize their success, wealth, or physical appearance to an extreme level. They may subtly or overtly imply that they're better than others, including you. If their bio or conversation is filled with talk about how great they are, how much they've accomplished, this could be a red flag.

They may steer conversations back to themselves, showing little interest or empathy in your thoughts or feelings. If they rarely ask about you, or when they do, it's superficial and they quickly move back to talking about themselves. They can frequently seek validation or compliments, often in subtle ways, like downplaying something about themselves to prompt praise from you.

Love Bombing is typical narcissistic behaviour, where they may shower you with excessive attention and flattery in the beginning, but this intensity can quickly fade once they feel they have you hooked. They might talk about an unrealistic or overly idealized future together very early on, and escalate the relationship quickly, using flattery or pressure to move things forward at a dizzying pace. I have had two dates who talked about wedding venues, marriage and holidays the following year after only a couple of dates, only to end the match a few weeks later.

They might try to dictate how the relationship should progress or manipulate your emotions to get what they want. They might be inconsistent in their communication or plans, putting you on the back foot and making themselves feel in control.

They may have strong opinions, expect you to cater to their needs or agree with them without question. I had a couple of conversations where men had very strong views of my social media presence (which I chose to ignore).

Look out for manipulative behaviour, such as gaslighting, which might include them subtly questioning your perceptions or making you doubt yourself. If you set a boundary, a narcissist might push back or try to make you feel guilty about asserting your needs or make you feel like you are asking something unreasonable.

These signs aren't definitive proof that someone is a narcissist, but if you notice several of these behaviours, it might be worth being cautious. Trust your instincts, and don't hesitate to set boundaries or walk away if something feels off.

THE MISOGYNIST

BIO

Name: *AlphaDave*

Age: *58 (but biologically superior to most men and all women)*

About Me: *Just a strong, traditional man looking for a woman who knows her place (hint: it's not the driver's seat). If you're into cooking, cleaning, and nodding along as I man-splain, we'll get on famously. Bonus points if you have "natural beauty" (but still wear makeup because I like it).*

What I experienced

This sounds fun but here are some lines from profiles I saw.

All I am looking for is a fun, busty bird, is that too much to ask?

If you wear heels you're a keeper.

Is there any fit not fat ladies left? Not into out of shape weirdos with tits.

How to spot a misogynist

How can you use your detective skills to see if your match is a misogynist when they are not necessarily overtly hostile toward women? There are certain red flags that can indicate you're dealing with a misogynist.

If their profile or conversation includes derogatory terms or jokes about women, even if they claim it's "just a joke," this is a clear red flag. Whether it's about women's bodies, sexuality, or roles in society it can indicate underlying misogynistic beliefs.

Look out for controlling behaviour. They might emphasise being an "alpha" or talk about traditional gender roles in a way that suggests they believe men should dominate women. One profile that sticks out, had in their bio that they insisted a woman had to wear stilettos not kitten heels for comfort on a date. Another said they would never date anyone over a size 10. They might focus on dating you to fulfill a certain image or to "prove" something about themselves.

If they insist on their opinions, especially about what women should or shouldn't do, and dismiss yours, this is a sign of a controlling attitude. They may minimize or dismiss women's achievements or suggest that certain professions or accomplishments are not suitable for women, or if they imply you are less knowledgeable or capable in certain areas simply because you're a woman.

If they use excessive sexual comments early in the conversation, or focus more on your physical appearance than on who you are as a person, this is a red flag. Watch out if their conversation or profile is heavily focused on looks, body types, or sexual attributes, it suggests they view women more as objects than people.

Look out for double standards. They may have different expectations for men and women, such as believing that men can date around while women should be "pure" or modest. Or criticise women for behaviours they wouldn't judge in men, such as being career-focused or sexually active. They might show respect for some women while speaking negatively about others, especially based on appearance, profession, or behaviour.

If they frequently interrupt you, talk over you, or seem disinterested when you speak, this suggests they don't value your opinions. Responding to your thoughts or feelings with dismissive or condescending comments is a sign of disrespect.

If they push you to do things you're not comfortable with or try to rush the relationship, this could indicate a sense of entitlement. They might get upset or impatient if you don't respond quickly, acting as though you owe them your time and attention.

Compliments that seem nice on the surface but demean other women (e.g., "You're not like other girls") can be a subtle form of misogyny. Making broad, generalised, negative statements about women, such as "all women are crazy," suggests deep-seated misogyny. If they talk negatively or blame all their exes for relationship problems, this can indicate a lack of respect for women and a refusal to take responsibility. I experienced this with a date and warning signs flashed up.

If they seem jealous or possessive early on, this could be a sign of controlling behaviour that often accompanies misogynistic attitudes. They might want to know who you're talking to or what you're always doing, which is a major red flag for potential abusive behaviour.

If they push past your boundaries, whether in conversation or in physical encounters, they're showing a lack of respect for your autonomy. If they continue to pursue you or act offended when you're not interested, this can indicate an inability to accept women's autonomy. If you encounter any of these signs, trust your instincts and proceed with caution. It's essential to prioritise your safety and well-being, both emotionally and physically, when interacting with someone new online.

THE MARRIED MAN

BIO

Name: *Single Steve (Don't Google Me) and sorry there are no profile photos*

Age: *45 (but my wedding photos add 5 years, so let's call it 50)*

About Me: *I'm just a busy professional looking for a bit of fun with someone who understands me, my wife doesn't. My perfect match is someone who doesn't ask too many questions—especially about my evening availability—and doesn't mind that I always keep my phone face-down. Bonus if you're good with code names in the contacts list.*

What I experienced

I had never thought about this before venturing on to dating apps, but it seems there's a lot of married men out there trying to meet partners for extra marital relationships.

There were three ways I saw that men tackled this.

Firstly, having no photos of themselves or cropped photos without showing their faces. They were looking for short-term fun or intimacy without commitment. I have no idea how this would be successful, as I am sure this faceless approach is not going to capture the imagination and desire of a woman looking for a match.

Secondly, being upfront in their bio. I guess you have to acknowledge their honesty there at least! Lines such as 'To be clear, I am not single' set out the lie of the land.

The last approach was using the line in their relationship goals "Looking for new friends" I connected with someone who looked to like the same outdoor activities as me. As we chatted, he asked what I was looking for. In return, he said he wanted to be honest, that he was married, but there was no real relationship, so he was looking outside of the marriage for a relationship. I asked if his wife knew. The answer? Nooo, she would kill me. That connection immediately ended but maybe it is something that works mutually for people looking for affairs. Sadly, the rise of dating apps has made these extramarital connections more accessible. The anonymity and convenience provided by these platforms can lower barriers to engaging in behaviour that might have previously required more effort and risk.

If a man's peers or colleagues use dating apps—even casually—this might normalize the behaviour, making them feel it's okay, "just flirting."

A dangerous game to play as I am sure they must get spotted at some point by people who know them.

So why take this risk?

The opportunity to chat to a total stranger who's looking for a spark, even for a short time, is an easy way for married men to seek validation and affirmation. If they are in long-term relationships, the excitement of early romance can fade. Dating apps offer instant gratification and an ego boost.

Routine and predictability in marriage can lead to boredom for some individuals and dating apps present a low-stakes way to escape this monotony. Engaging with unsuspecting women looking to date might offer a sense of adventure or novelty they feel they are missing out on.

Some married men may feel that their physical or sexual needs are not being met in their marriage. Instead of addressing these issues openly, they can now resort to dating apps to fulfil these desires discreetly. They can rationalize their actions to themselves.

They might see it as harmless fun or believe that since they are not physically cheating, their actions do not constitute betrayal.

And then there's the notorious 'midlife crisis'. Feelings of inadequacy or a fear of aging, can have men seeking external validation. The attention they receive from younger or different women might temporarily soothe their insecurities.

While motivations vary, the consequences of this behaviour are often significant. Trust, a cornerstone of any marriage, is being damaged. Even if interactions on a dating app do not lead to a physical affair, the emotional betrayal can be just as hurtful. For the spouse, if they discover such activity it can result in feelings of inadequacy, betrayal, and anger. For a single woman looking for a single partner, being led on by a married man can be really damaging. In most instances single people going on an app are not looking to find a partner that's already married. If they feel attracted, only to discover the match is married, that can also cause feelings of betrayal, loss, lack of self-worth and guilt. If you have any suspicions, it's worth asking the question to put your mind at rest.

THE THREESOME HOPEFUL

BIO

Name: *Eric Plus-One*

Age: *We are 53 (and 51) but open to all ages as long as you're "adventurous"*

About Me: *Couples' therapist by day, crowd pleaser by night. My partner and I are just exploring, and we're looking for someone confident, open-minded, and willing to have fun. Not your thing? No worries—just don't knock it till you've tried it (with us). Swipe right to join our "team"!*

What I experienced

This was an unexpected category to crop up on Bumble, but on a busy dating app, with enough people, the odds must be someone will say yes.

The give-away was the profile pic, of the man with his partner, often described as his hot wife. As I had said that I was looking for a male partner, the application submitted must have meant they were only on the hunt for a female to join them.

If it's your thing

Call it a threesome, a throuple or a triad, this is something that's popular and well documented both historically and romantically.

If all parties are willing participants then no harm is done. The nature of being on a dating app as a woman looking for a male partner and being approached like this meant that the combination being sought was 2 women with one man, but all sorts of combinations can apply and there are apps specifically aimed at enabling threesomes if that's what you want.

THE FANTASIST

BIO

Name: *Sir Lancelot of LinkedIn*

Age: *48 (but I was a Viking warrior in a past life)*

About Me: *Billionaire entrepreneur. Part-time secret agent. Full-time genius. I once almost climbed Everest, nearly got cast in a major Hollywood film, and technically have royal blood (a distant duke, but it counts). Looking for someone who can keep up with my incredibly real adventures and doesn't ask too many follow-up questions.*

What I experienced

Ah, this character is going to get a whole chapter to themselves... as I managed to fall for someone who turned out to be just this and more...

CHAPTER 8
THE FANTASIST
(OR ROMANCE SCAMMER, YOU DECIDE)

So I will premise this with how I would watch stories of how many women (and men) are sadly often conned by people out of money by romance frauds and I'd wonder how they could be so gullible. Thankfully, at the time of writing this, I have had nothing like that happen, but my ego, my trust in human nature and my confidence in online dating took a huge knock with this character. I am still unsure whether at best, this man was a complete fantasist trying to impress me, or at worst, a romance scammer who I found the truth about in time! I am actually quite embarrassed to share this, but I hope that it shows how if a smart, switched on woman can be deceived for 8 weeks, despite so many red flags and queries from friends, then it can happen to many people. I still don't know how much of what I heard from him were lies or the truth, and I don't think I ever will. I fell in love with him as he inundated me with the affection that I needed. I still want to believe that it was real, but he may have been the best actor in the world and has left a wake of women he's deceived behind him. Read, take note and don't let it happen to you.

As I was testing different apps, someone had suggested I try Tinder. Sadly, they were 99% men I would never be attracted to. I tried to be open minded and read profiles to get beyond looks, but didn't see anyone until James (who we'll re-name for the purpose of this chapter) popped up.

Good-looking and smiling – tick

Twinkling, kind blue eyes – tick

Full length pic with cute chocolate labrador – tick

A bio that had some character – tick

And only 35 miles away?

Bingo! A match it was.

During just one day of chatting on the app where we had lots of interaction and communication which I was thrilled with (it is one of my non-negotiables), we exchanged numbers.

With great conversation flowing, we agreed to a video call immediately (as I've mentioned, something I did without fail to ensure someone looked and sounded like their profile).

His first words as I saw him were "Wow, you're beautiful!" as if he couldn't help himself, which was very endearing and flattering. Our chat was fun and easy and we agreed to a date.

As we discussed our interests, I mentioned that I painted.

James mentioned he did pencil drawings as a hobby and sent me 25 pictures of his pencil drawings, from quick sketches to the most phenomenal photo realistic portraits. I was blown away by how talented he was. He said he had lots more, but couldn't share with me due to client confidentiality as he did commissions.

As date day came, he sent me a photo from his car, and I was pinching myself as he looked gorgeous. I thought it was just for me and was excited to meet him. What I was soon to find out was that he had a library of photos that he kept dipping into, that weren't taken in the moment.

From the second we met in the pub car park, we were like a couple of teenagers, giggly, flirty, chatting incessantly about everything, finding reasons to brush hands, and yes, eventually sharing a kiss.

I was surprised at the level of detail and candidness about some of his previous dates (mostly how mad the women were, or how they had had misleading pictures online) and how his previous relationships had ended. **This is a narcissistic trait – to always put the blame on other people,** more of which were to manifest. However, at the time I liked his openness and as I tend to wear my heart on my sleeve, I loved meeting someone willing to share experiences.

As a first date goes, it was amazing, we didn't want the evening to end and it was followed up swiftly with trying to organise another date. As I was going away on holiday a week later we arranged a lunch for the day I was leaving.

In the interim his messages told me he had never believed in love at first sight, but after meeting me he did and if he'd been paired with me on *Married at First Sight,* he'd have leapt at the chance to say "I do". He'd told his friends all about me, and how he'd never felt this way after one date. He said that I was the most beautiful woman he'd ever dated and that I deserved someone better than him. I instantly replied with compliments and told him that he was not to say that again. This turned out to happen often, with James looking for constant attention and reassurance. As our second date loomed, he said he needed more than just lunch with me and wanted to spend the whole day with me before I left for my holiday that evening. He said he would take the day off work for me. I, of course, was very flattered.

He also wanted to make a pact with me that we would both say what we felt without guard which, as a trusting and open person, I was up for, but this meant he could learn to manipulate me from my responses.

For our second date, we walked around a local beauty spot, hand in hand, talking and kissing. As we walked, he was asking what had gone wrong with my previous relationship. As I described needing good communication and to feel appreciated, he was starting to gain chinks in my armour to woo me later on. He showered me with compliments and was a complete gentleman making sure he bought lunch. He must have told me how beautiful I was about 20 times on the date and how he couldn't believe how perfect I was for him. This was the beginning of the **love bombing.**

Straight from the date, I drove down to Norfolk to meet Michelle, my matchmaker friend for a few days away. I described how I had been swept off my feet, but that it all seemed to be happening too fast with talk of marriage and love already. I know I am a hopeless romantic and meeting someone as passionate as me was heady stuff.

She suggested slowing the relationship down to get to know each other better, but when I suggested this to him, he started to withdraw, saying I was confusing him and "shouldn't we just go with our own feelings?" As he was backing away, and I was drawn to him, I agreed. This is a classic way that narcissists **manipulate your feelings,** blowing hot, then cold. It was a pattern that would repeat itself.

On our next date, he would be joining me in London for a day out. We chatted excitedly on the phone or on text about things we could do. The evening before, he went strangely quiet. I got a long message from him saying it was never going to work out between us, that I was too successful and fit for him and that he was already falling in love with me. He knew we would end as I was bound to meet someone more appropriate. He said our lifestyles were too different, we come from different worlds. I reassured him with the famous clip from Notting Hill where Julia Roberts tells Hugh Grant she's just a girl standing in front of a boy, asking him to love her. I convinced him to come to London for our third date.

I went back saying I was not materialistic, his salary didn't matter, it's all about the person inside for me. After a lot of me convincing him that we had enjoyed two great dates that showed so much promise, and that we should see how date three went, he agreed to come to London. This was the start of regular messages from him that created a drama that required me to keep assuring him of my affection. A narcissistic trait known as **hoovering and discarding.**

We had the most fabulous day at art galleries, eating fresh seafood and walking in Regents Park. As we chatted at the galleries, we talked about his art and how he wanted to make more of that as a career. Whilst together, we bought a domain name under his name, as a goal for the future. An aspiration for when it could be his full-time occupation instead of web design which was what he was doing now.

He shared his business website, saying not to judge as it needed updating. For someone whose job it was to design websites for others, it was uninspiring and basic, but I didn't want to comment as we had just got over him saying he wasn't good enough for me. I read the strategy of how his process worked, but there were no design examples. He offered to design me a website to promote my book and my consulting, but as he always seemed busy and had art commissions to finish, I said to focus on those instead.

He shared his dating history with me; two marriages and three long-term relationships.

All of them seemed to have some kind of drama attached to them.

The first marriage broke up post his time in the army as he married young and as he left he knew he'd changed. Two long relationships had ended with another woman turning his girlfriends against him, one of whom was his sister. That girlfriend had burnt all photos of him as a child, so he had none, as well all his artwork. He said he had nothing of his history to survive from the relationship. This was maybe another sign that he'd be difficult to trace as things developed.

His last 6-year relationship had ended bitterly, and he'd put a lot financially into a joint property. He was still haggling through the courts to get £350,000 from her, which was his share. This was due to him, with a cut-off date of end November, 4 months after we met.

He relayed another drama, of one of his friends letting him know in the pub that someone he vaguely knew was using his photos on a Facebook profile to meet women. He said he'd contacted the guy, furious and it had been taken down. Only now looking back with new information, I realise this was probably him using a fake identity to meet other women. He often asked me what I liked about his photos, or him, no doubt to adapt his chameleon existence.

We continued to see each other more and more, enjoying nights in, days out, country walks, pub lunches as well as him helping with mundane tasks like taking recycling cardboard boxes to the tip and DIY jobs around my house. He was really kind and supportive in every way. He started talking about plans in the future which felt a long way out to me, given the relationship was only three weeks old. He asked me to be his plus one at a wedding in December (this was in August) and booked the hotel room for us. His dream was to have a camper van and travel the UK, Europe and America and asked if I would choose it with him.

As I had told him I had never had a holiday planned for me, he said he wanted to take me away to see the new year in, together, could I free my diary from 29th December to 3rd January? Of course I could! How romantic was this? He said he'd need my passport details to book a flight and shared his passport with me. I didn't know at the time, but these long-term plans are all **subtle ways of tying you into the relationship.**

It seemed we were both smitten and yes, though early days, had fallen in love. The all-consuming, free-spirited kind found the start of a relationship. This is an exciting time, as you get to know each other. After a marriage where my ex found it difficult to declare love, it was intoxicating. Both working alone and living alone, we chatted frequently and kept each other company physically and virtually. I was told how much he loved me over and over, how he missed me when I wasn't there, and he called me 2–3 times per day. What happens with love bombing like this, is it becomes a norm, so if it stops, or you get a message that's critical, you think something's wrong. You want to work hard to get the relationship back to how it was, and people pleasing behaviour kicks in. This happened quite frequently, leaving me wondering about his mood swings. In relaying to friends how this had happened a couple of times, they flagged that it seemed unusual to behave in such an extreme, emotional way, especially so early on, and that the erratic hot and cold behaviour was a red flag, but by this stage I was hooked.

He told me that being with me, despite him already being active, regularly walking his chocolate Labrador, I had inspired him to improve his fitness and diet. He was thrilled as it was already helping his diabetes and body confidence. As a very handsome man, he hated the slight middle aged spread he'd been getting, and he kept telling me how grateful he was. It felt good to have made a difference to someone's health and self-esteem.

He sent me more and more of his art to look at, some dating back over 20 years as well as showing me the professional pencil kit he had. It contained hundreds of pencils which he said were his addiction, along with the new CAD design equipment he'd got for his web design work. I got more and more excited about him being able to step away from doing websites and creating a career out of doing what he loved, the photo realistic portrait and erotic pencil drawings. He said the beginning of 2025 was his goal to make this happen.

When we visited a gallery, part of a chain, he said he was an artist and showed them his work. They said he must e-mail some of his work to the gallery owners. We excitedly chatted about which pieces he should send. That evening, I sent two or three of his pieces to a friend who worked with the company. She came back instantly, blown away by his work, as I was. She enthusiastically said how talented he was and she would speak to the owners. I messaged him to share the great news and instantly got a phone call back. He said he wasn't angry, but he had signed NDAs with clients, and I shouldn't have sent work without checking with him first as it could cause him problems. He'd only shared it with me as I was his girlfriend. He told me to give him a couple of weeks to sort out his work, and he would send. I was hugely disappointed but deleted the photos from the conversation with my friend and let her know what was going to happen. Despite me mentioning following up with the gallery to James a couple of times, the edited version of his work never materialised as he said he was too busy with web design work and drawing commissions.

As his 20-year-old daughter was living with him at home before going to university, he always came to my house to see me, as we both agreed it was early days to be introducing each other to our families. Even when his daughter left to go to university, James always suggested coming to see me.

I often suggested meeting him halfway. He always said it was no problem to drive to me, with him only being an hour away. His elderly mother and sister lived not far from me, so it was convenient for him to visit them from me, it made sense. Two good friends queried why I hadn't been to see him, but his reasons seemed fair enough to me.

About three weeks into the romance, whilst we were out on a walk two miles away from my home, he was suddenly in a lot of pain. White and shaking, he took me by both hands and said we needed to get back. He hadn't wanted to tell me, but he was being investigated for bowel cancer. We rushed back to my house, where he rushed upstairs, texting me saying he felt terrible and should probably go. I was extremely sympathetic, despite being rather knocked for six by this news and, of course, offered comfort, but wanted to know more. Part of me was wondering how I had managed to start dating someone who knew they were under investigation for cancer, but as I didn't want to overthink, parked those thoughts. He explained he'd been having stomach problems for six months but had only had bowel screenings in the last month.

He let me know he had various tests planned over the next couple of weeks, blood tests and colonoscopies.

As I am a great believer in not overthinking, I wasn't going to ponder too much about the future of our budding relationship until the tests came back.

In sharing this news with my closest friends, they were shocked that someone who knew they were going through these tests, with the possible impact on their life, had started dating someone through a dating app. I asked him if he knew, and he said he'd thought it may be a reaction to new diabetes drugs when he'd started dating me and, at this stage, I believed him. As someone who has always been kind, I wanted to help James one way or another to deal with this, even if it did mean as a friend.

If this was not enough going on, week four of our dating, I was due to go on a solo holiday in Italy. Just as I was getting ready to travel, he let me know his mum had collapsed and had been rushed to hospital with sepsis.

His messages became cold and one word. His way of coping with difficulty was to do it alone and if I pushed him too much to help, he would push me away. After a very difficult day, and it being the second time he'd dramatically changed his behaviour pattern with me, I decided I couldn't cope with the roller coaster of extreme emotions I was on the receiving end of. Not just blowing hot and cold, but going from molten lava to glacial.

The next time I saw him I said we needed to talk seriously. I was putting in place boundaries and felt proud of myself. I let him know that twice in four weeks, he'd had a complete switch in behaviour and communication, that had left me feeling confused and anxious. I wanted consistency and no game playing so if it happened a third time it would mean the end of us. He explained that the first time was genuinely that he felt there could be no future for us having such different lifestyles and financial background, but I had convinced him that that was not a blocker for us. The second time was the stress of a cancer diagnosis and his mum being ill, and he was trying to push me away, as he was struggling to deal with all of it himself. I agreed these were good reasons, but reiterated that it didn't change how I felt about inconsistent behavior. He took that on the chin and said it wouldn't happen again.

My good friend did start to ask what proof did I have that his mother was ill or indeed was he really ill himself. I dismissed the questions as 'who would possibly fake something so awful?'

A few days later I left for Italy. He bought a sketch pad and pencils as a gift to take so that I could practise my pencil drawing to show him, and he would teach me more when I got back.

As I was trying to relax and enjoy the holiday, I was getting messages of his mother being told she only had a few days to live. What was supposed to be a few days, dragged into weeks with his mother rallying around, then fading, only to rally around again. Over the next couple of weeks, he lived at the hospital, or at his sisters who lived near to their mother. He was hard to get hold of as signal was poor in the hospital. He was struggling to do his regular work as he couldn't use his PC at home, only having a laptop on him. I offered several times to take him things he needed at the hospital or to meet him for a coffee outside but he said no. He managed to get over to me once during this time which he said was a well needed reprieve from all of the stress.

Over the next few weeks he had his various tests. Whilst we had time together, he suffered, sometimes from nausea, fatigue and said he'd had a couple of nosebleeds. Although we continued to carry on as normal, we did start to talk about what we should do, as it was confirmed cancer cells were detected. James asked if I thought I would stay with him through the treatment as he would rather end our relationship now, than me leave him halfway through. This question, six weeks into a relationship felt like a lot of pressure. I am not a shallow person and the intensity of feelings in only a few weeks meant I felt torn. Newly single, the last thing I would have chosen for a new partnership was to see someone through six months of chemotherapy that could make them very ill. I am someone who will not over promise and underdeliver, so I replied honestly, that I couldn't promise this so soon. I have elderly parents to look after, a divorce to navigate, a daughter starting IVF, and could only say we could take each challenge as it came. He responded badly saying he needed to know one way or the other.

Pragmatically, I said we should wait to find out how bad the diagnosis is, and how long and arduous the treatment was going to be.

My friends meanwhile were urging me to let the relationship end, that it was unfair of him to expect to see him through cancer treatment after only six weeks. He told me his friends were advising the same.

Within a week, the diagnosis and treatment plan came back. It was bad news. He had Non-Hodgkins lymphoma, a blood cancer and an aggressive variant. The treatment would be a very strong course of chemotherapy that would start the following week. He called me via a video call to tell me, as he knew it would be hard in person. He said knowing this, he was making the call that we should end or at least stall our relationship as it would be too hard for us to deal with and maintain a new romance. Both tearful, we agreed a break, or a lull at least. We would catch up monthly as an update on how he was.

As he was due to attend the first event with me as a plus one the weekend before he started his chemo, we decided we would go all out to make it a weekend to remember.

We had our last two days and nights together. The first evening was very emotional. I had bought him a book to fill with adventures we could have together. It was to give him, and us, hope and dreams for after his treatment. We wrote down a place per page, from Paris, to Switzerland, to the US, that he said he would illustrate. He filmed me cooking for him, flirting to the camera, Nigella Lawson style, and dancing around the kitchen. He took lots of photos, as he wanted to draw me, and send it to me as a present.

In tears, he told me I was the best thing that had happened to him in his life, and he didn't want to lose me.

The next day I had to go out for two meetings, so I left James at my house to do some DIY jobs he'd offered to do. I returned about 3pm and we both got glammed up for a meal out which was my treat as an early birthday present for him as we wouldn't be able to spend it together. We then went on to my friend's 50th birthday party at a club where it was a joy to be together, dancing and laughing.

On returning to my house we sat and listened to music that made us laugh or conjured up moments we two had shared together. making a joint playlist. We made the evening last as long as we could knowing he'd be leaving the next morning and we wouldn't see each other for at least six months at best, or possibly never again. He made sure I had his home address and email so I could post him a birthday card and send him updates, and he asked for my email and birthday date too.

The next morning, delaying as long as possible as he had to leave to see his daughter before he started chemo, we said a very emotional goodbye.

Despite our decision to only speak once a month, we had agreed that he would speak to me at the end of the week after his first chemo session just to let me know how it was. After this, we failed miserably at not talking, updating each other often with news. A week later we had a video call to reassess how we'd stay in touch. I suggested a weekly video call, which James leapt on, and declared he'd been worried if we didn't talk regularly, he'd lose me with the lack of communication. That was the last thing in the world he wanted. The only thought that would get him through the next six months was seeing me at the end of it.

A few days later I went to the theatre in London with one of the closest friends.

As we travelled back we chatted about James and she, along with my other close friends, asked how I was sure I knew all he'd been saying was true? The fact I'd never been to see his house, how did I not know if he was married? How was I sure that his mother had been ill, could he have been on a family holiday? As she was asking questions it made me realise how many strange events had happened, which individually were ok, but added up in the space of eight weeks were suspicious.

Even as we were talking, I got a message to say he'd been rushed to A&E as his blood glucose levels were sky high due to his nausea and inability to eat properly with the chemo drugs.

As budding detectives, we decided I would drive up to his house the next morning and park up and watch to see if a) he was married b) he was as ill as he said he was. A plan was hatched and I arranged with my father to borrow his car the following morning so that he wouldn't recognise mine.

As I arrived home that evening, my mind whirring, I wanted to see where I was going and searched for it on Google Maps but the address couldn't be found. I kept trying and eventually by typing it into Google I found it was the registered address for a company we'll call Andrew's Construction. This seemed odd, but I knew he rented so it was possible that he rented from them.

Next, I went to look at his website to see if there was an address, only to find that it had been closed and the domain was not taken. The registered business address for his company was still his old home address from five years ago on the South Coast. With my stomach churning, all sorts of thoughts were starting to go through my mind. I went to bed knowing I was going to drive up to see his home the following day. I decided to reverse photo search the art he'd sent to me as his. Many had his signature on. The first one I searched popped straight up with a different artist's name. I did another and that one popped up with a completely different artist's name. At this stage there was no stopping and I was awake for nearly two hours researching. I found out of the 40 pieces of art he'd sent to me, including ones where I had heard him give vivid descriptions to gallery owners about the sitter, at least 30 were traceable to 30 different artists.

This deception had started day 1 of us chatting and had carried on building week after week. I felt horrified, scared, embarrassed and desperately sad.

It was damning evidence.

I waited till 9am then grabbed a long, dark wig from my fancy dress drawer and a baseball cap (I could have found a new vocation!) and went and exchanged my car for my fathers. I set off for the address he'd given me, an hours drive north of me.

As I got closer, I put on the wig and cap and then drove slowly around the crescent. It was on a small new build estate and there was nowhere I could park and watch. I drove past the address though and parked on the drive was a white van and small black car- neither of which matched the two cars I knew he drove.

I circled around and as I did a young man came out of the house and drove off in the van. I knew James didn't have a son so this was suspicious.

I decided to park up and go and knock on the door.

With heart pounding, and knees shaking, I approached the house. I peered into the kitchen window to see if it looked like the house

I'd seen on video calls and as I did three little white dogs started jumping up and barking. James had a chocolate labrador so this was another warning sign. A woman's face appeared at the window and so I smiled and went to knock on the door. As she answered the door, I apologised and said with a forced smile on my face, "I think I may have the wrong address, does James live here?" The answer was "No, no-one called James lives here." I smiled, apologised again and left to return to my car, a sense of panic arising. In the meantime James had been messaging wondering why I hadn't answered his message about the hospital visit the night before. I made up an excuse about being with my parents while I was wondering what to do.

As I drove home I had all sorts of thoughts going through my head – I'd left someone who was seemingly a complete liar and potential romance scammer alone in my house for six hours only a few days before in complete trust. He had my passport details, my email, had been on my laptop, and I remembered then that my driving license had gone missing whilst I had been seeing him.

When I got home I leapt straight on to my laptop to go over again how I might be able to track him down as he had deleted all social media accounts including LinkedIn. Despite trying every avenue to find more on James, we all hit dead ends. As a tech expert he had done an impressive job of hiding his traces.

I searched the internet asking what to do if you feel you have come across a romance scam and it said to contact the police.

At this stage I felt I needed advice, so called the local police force at 8pm.

They were unbelievably supportive and helpful, and when I went through the list of lies, deleted accounts, details he'd asked for, they agreed it was all very suspicious and gave me a crime number. They took his passport details and said not to alert him to the fact I had spoken to them, to carry on conversations as normal. I quickly got a phone call back to say that his passport was real and he had no convictions or reports against him. With this news, I felt a slight sense of relief that at least he was a real person and hadn't faked their ID. Their advice was to let the relationship fizzle, but I still needed to feel secure. This man had lied repeatedly to me to win my heart and deceive me, and I needed to know more.

Still in mild shock and denial, but with this news, I decided to confront James with the first of his lies, the undeniable fact he'd given me a false address.

I dropped him a message to say that I was sorry that I'd not been communicative, but as he was so ill, I'd decided to visit him at his home to make sure he was okay. On arrival at the address he'd given me, on speaking to the owner, it was 100% clear he didn't live there – what explanation did he have?

There was a long pause. His answer was another obvious lie, pulled out of the hat.

Even though only three days before he'd wanted a weekly call with me so he wouldn't lose me, his excuse was that he had given me the wrong address on purpose as he knew, for sure, he was walking away that day. He said our relationship needed to be over, and he thought that was the best way – I didn't need him and his poor health and financial problems, so he wanted to make sure he was going out of my life forever. It was all to 'protect me', as he 'loved me so much'. At this stage he didn't know that I'd found he'd faked all of his art and deleted his existence from everything online.

I said how very sad that was, if that's how he felt, I would take it that this was the end but could he still gift me the drawing he had been doing of me. He'd said it was almost finished and I asked if I could at least see a photo to keep me going.

After a lot of stalling, saying it wasn't finished or that he was too ill to get it from his office, he sent me the 'drawing' which was very obviously just a black and white filter on a photo he had taken of me.

If I hadn't been so shell shocked by the deceit, it would have been laughable. As I didn't reply, he quickly deleted it saying I must not like it as I hadn't commented.

I replied I had been on a call and could he resend.

This time he sent as a Whatsapp vanishing photo, with a long message about how it had taken hours, he was so proud of it, and it was 'so good it was untrue'. A clever play on words, as I believe he knew I was on to him.

He asked for my thoughts. My thoughts at the time were still horrified that a man who had so much detail on me, was untraceable. I decided I would just play along and said it looked great and looked forward to receiving it. I wanted to buy myself more time to do detective work and ensure I was safe from any fraud.

I spent the next day cancelling and replacing my passport, driving license. I changed all my bank logins. I checked my laptop for any spyware. I looked back over my doorbell camera history to ensure there was no way James could have had a key cut for my house.

SO WHAT DID I DO NEXT...?

Having made sure all my finances, data, property and documents were as secure as I could, I decided to just let the connection drift.

I have no idea what James's intentions were.

Is he a fantasist who wanted to impress me? Does he really have cancer? Or is he a liar and romance scammer who not only lied about his art, his address, his company and website, he also lied about his mother's illness and his own cancer. Was he after a loan towards the £350,000 he was unlikely to get from his ex and did I make a lucky escape? I always want to think the best of people, and I genuinely fell in love with James, and still want to believe he did me, but as I relay the story here as I have shared with my friends previously, sadly I am convinced of the latter.

CHAPTER 9
THE FIRST DATE

I hope that last chapter hasn't put you off. I have to stress, in amongst the red flags and swipe fatigue, dating can be fun.

So let's assume, after your requirements have been hit and your checks are complete, a match has got through.

I now want to talk through managing that first date.

PLAN THE IDEAL DATE

When it comes to meeting in person, you need to think about the ideal first date for you. This means choosing a place, time and activity that is going to make you feel as comfortable and at ease as possible.

I always suggested meeting around 6.30pm with a view that you should try to give a date an hour, especially if you've both had to drive any distance to meet. The timing meant if the date felt it had run its natural course in an hour, 7.30pm was a good time to say you had to leave for dinner and not feel too awkward cutting it short. If you choose a venue or activity that will allow you to extend the date if you wish, this gives you flexibility.

For example, while bike rides or bowling might be fun ideas, if these aren't your usual activities don't use a first date as an excuse to try out a new hobby. Instead, pick something simple, perhaps just going for a drink in a relatively quiet and lowkey place where you have the chance to talk and get to know each other with the flexibility to extend the date should you both be enjoying one another's company.

It's been interesting to see the growth of non-drinkers, as this opens different opportunities for that first meeting instead of a bar. I've done walking dates with a coffee, which is a really lovely way to meet someone. From a personal perspective I love walking and you have the benefit of outside stimulus to talk about.

WEAR SOMETHING THAT MAKES YOU FEEL GOOD

With my background in fashion (37 years starting as a designer) I am very confident in how I put clothes together. But being back on the dating scene did make me think more about what to wear than normal. Would I look too staid or too sexy? Would I look overdressed if they turned up casual? I then decided to stop myself in my over-thinking tracks and decided that I would just wear something that made me feel fabulous and confident.

Much like choosing a new activity is not ideal for a first date, my main tip is don't use this opportunity to wear something new that could make you feel uncomfortable or self-conscious. The last thing you want to be thinking about is whether your skirt is too short or your waistband is digging in. You don't want to be fiddling around with your clothes all night. When you are uncomfortable it shows in your body language and can be misinterpreted as lack of interest by your date – which could be miles from the truth.

Don't be afraid to wear colour, it can be a real mood booster. Red is the colour for confidence, pink for feeling romantic and blue is calming. Colours can make you stand out from the crowd in more ways than one.

DISCUSS LIFESTYLE, INTERESTS AND ASPIRATIONS

Hopefully you have covered a lot of this off in your chats and video call before meeting, but it's a good chance to expand on what you've learned about your date up to then.

Talk about your daily routines, hobbies, and interests. It's important that your lifestyles are compatible or that you're willing to accommodate each other. It's worth considering how much of your life you want to keep independent and pursue your own interests and how much you like to share activities. I discovered with one match that although we had the most incredible dates, he wanted me to fit around a very busy work schedule and existing friendship groups and only wanted to date every ten days to two weeks. It was fun for a few dates, but I realised I wanted a couple of dates per week, and time at weekends, so long term I knew it wasn't going to be a relationship. My family are very important to me, and spending time with them is a joy. For me establishing whether a future partner was caring about their family was essential.

COMMUNICATION AND BODY LANGUAGE

I believe interested people are interesting. Meeting someone in real life is a chance to see how they communicate. An enjoyable date with flowing conversation requires two way dialogue, which needs listening skills. You need to be able to discuss different topics. If you have different views on things, and I am sure there will be some areas where you won't agree, pay attention to how they handle it. Are they open minded? Are they dogmatic? If you can constructively handle differences, this is a sign of a mature and compatible partner.

Body language on a first date can provide a lot of valuable insight into their level of interest, confidence, and emotional state. Subtle cues, such as posture, gestures, and facial expressions, can reveal what the conversation may not.

As an example, there is some evidence to say holding a warm cup such as coffee can make your behaviour warmer.

One key indicator is posture. A man who sits upright, leans slightly forward, and angles his body toward you is likely engaged and interested. This openness suggests attentiveness and a desire to connect. Conversely, crossed arms, slouching, or turning away can indicate discomfort, disinterest, or nervousness.

Eye contact is another important signal. Prolonged eye contact demonstrates confidence and attentiveness, showing he's focused on you. However, if his gaze repeatedly shifts to his surroundings, he might be distracted or not fully invested in the conversation. Having said that, eye contact could signal shyness so bear that in mind, as it may improve through the date.

Gestures can also speak volumes. Fidgeting or repeatedly touching his face, neck, or hands might suggest nervousness or insecurity, especially if he's trying to make a good impression. Meanwhile, mirroring your movements—subconsciously mimicking your gestures—can indicate rapport and genuine interest. Subtle touches, like brushing his hand against yours or leaning closer, could suggest he feels comfortable and is testing boundaries to establish a deeper connection.

Look at how they smile. A genuine smile that reaches his eyes shows warmth and sincerity. If it feels forced, it may be insincere.

Take all of this into context. Your date may naturally exhibit nervous or reserved behaviour without it reflecting their level of interest. Balance the conversation with the body language to get a better understanding of his intentions and feelings.

PAYING THE BILL

Having discussed this with others this is a controversial topic!

My take on this is that as I am financially independent, would not choose an expensive venue for a first date, and expect to be treated as equal in other situations, I offer to split the bill. I personally felt that I then had no obligation to my date. If I had a date that I thought I'd definitely see again and he insisted on paying? I would acquiesce knowing other dates would follow where I could share costs.

If you know there's a big difference in incomes between you, I would re-consider my stance here.

BUT, I have encountered strong opinions, based on tradition, from both men and women who felt that the gentleman should always pay. One friend said she would never go on a second date with a man who wanted to split the bill.

Michelle, with her experience in relationship counselling, has the view that you should sit back and see what the man does. Let him lead so he doesn't feel emasculated.

I've bounced this off a couple of male friends, who are very comfortable in their own skin, and they didn't have this as a concern.

I think this is one of those areas with a lot of nuances; the person, the meeting place, the cost and whether you think there will be a second date. Based on these you make a judgement call that feels right at the time.

CHAPTER 10

WHEN TO GET INTIMATE?

The next big question which seems to play on every woman's mind that I've spoken to, is deciding when to take your relationship to the next level. Especially when coming out of a long relationship.

The inner dialogue is;

"Am I ready?"

"Is it too soon?"

"Will he think I am too easy/not interested in sex?"

"Will it change things?"

"What will he think of my body?"

The truth is, there's no one-size-fits-all answer, there is no "right" or "wrong" time. The decision is deeply personal and varies for everyone. Try to avoid the noise of others' opinions and reflect on what's right for you. You may be someone looking for, as the apps put it, "Intimacy without commitment" or you may be looking for a long-term, monogamous relationship.

The reality is that every relationship is unique, the decision is very personal, and the pace at which intimacy develops should reflect the needs and values of both partners. What's most important is that the decision feels right to you both and is made with mutual consent and understanding.

The timing of intimacy is not just about physical connection; it's also about emotional readiness, mutual respect, the stage of your relationship and what you want from it. For some, there's instant physical chemistry. The spark ignites quickly, with a strong, instant connection. However, if the connection is built on strong physical attraction or lust, rather than a deeper emotional bond, it can be short lived.

For others, intimacy may evolve more slowly, requiring time to build trust and emotional depth. Recognising where you, and your new partner, are on this spectrum can help guide your decision.

AM I READY?

Before anything else, ask yourself: am I emotionally and physically ready? If you've come out of a long relationship, intimacy with someone new might feel daunting or complicated. If you're not sure, it's perfectly okay to wait. Sexual intimacy is meaningful when you're truly ready for it, not when you feel pressured by timelines or expectations.

If you are wanting a longer term, more meaningful relationship, before becoming intimate, it's essential to assess your emotional readiness. Are you comfortable with your partner? Do you trust them? Emotional readiness means being in a place where you feel secure in your connection and confident that intimacy will deepen your relationship rather than complicate it. If you're still feeling unsure or anxious about the relationship, it might be wise to take more time to get to know each other.

Communication is key. Have open, honest conversations with your partner about your feelings, expectations, and boundaries. This dialogue not only ensures that both of you are on the same page but also strengthens your emotional bond, laying a solid foundation for a healthy relationship.

Some people might place a high value on waiting until they feel a strong emotional or even spiritual connection, while others may feel comfortable moving forward based on physical attraction and mutual respect. There's no one-size-fits-all approach, but it's crucial to align your actions with what feels right for you.

Ultimately, you know yourself best. Trust your instincts. If it feels right, it probably is. If it doesn't feel right, don't ignore that inner voice.

IS IT TOO SOON?

Sexual intimacy thrives on trust. If you're dating someone new, focus on building emotional connection and mutual understanding first. Make sure they respect your boundaries and that the relationship feels secure. Feeling safe and valued creates the foundation for a fulfilling sexual relationship.

If you're unsure whether the time is right, consider the level of trust you've established with your partner. Do you feel confident that they respect your boundaries and will honour your needs? If the answer is yes, you're in a good place to take the next step. If not, then consider taking the relationship a little slower and giving you both that extra time for trust to develop. There's no deadline for intimacy, remember: sex isn't a milestone you need to rush toward.

WILL HE THINK I AM TOO EASY/NOT INTERESTED IN SEX?

So we are older, more experienced and feel freer from the pressures of youth—but societal norms can still linger. Some may urge you to "take it slow" while others suggest you should "let loose." Forget the noise. What matters is your comfort and the pace that feels right for you and your relationship.

WILL IT CHANGE THINGS?

It may seem an embarrassing topic to bring up, but it's important to communicate openly.

When the time feels right, talk honestly with your new partner about your feelings and expectations. Discuss contraception, sexual health, and any concerns (there is a rise in STDs amongst the over 50's, so it's important to get over any embarrassment to protect your health!). You also need to be clear whether the relationship is monogamous or not and agree to the boundaries that this stage brings.

Recognise that sex can bring complications. Sex introduces emotional depth into the relationship. Be mindful of whether you're seeking sex to deepen your bond, or if it's purely physical. Reflect on whether you're prepared for the emotional changes intimacy may bring.

WHAT WILL HE THINK OF MY BODY?

First and foremost, if you have worked on your self-love, self confidence and self-esteem before starting to date, you should recognise you are a wonderful package! This is what men will see.

If you have built a strong connection, with trust and respect before you get intimate, the relationship is not just based on the physical.

And remember, you have had a few dates. Your partner is going to know your size and shape, so you will not be completely surprised by how you look as you remove your clothes. They may have the same concerns themselves. Don't overthink, just embrace the moment.

CHAPTER 11
THE FUNNIEST DATING STORIES

Well, along with my escapades, it seems there are a lot of tales to tell.

I asked friends and connections on social media to share anything that would make for an interesting or illuminating story and wow, have they delivered.

I want to thank the ladies who shared stories and there are a lot of common themes as well as some unique incidents. I haven't shared any names or correct locations to keep these anonymous.

I had been chatting to a nice guy for a few days. He was obviously a gym go-er as had included very muscled topless photos in his bio. After initial pleasantries, I got sent a d*ck pic with the main item blacked out and an offer to see a video of him with his previous girlfriend having sex to see how well endowed he was! BLOCKED!

I met up with a guy on Tinder once. When I met him, he seemed vaguely familiar. After a few drinks, it came to me. I am a beauty therapist and used to do his back, sack and crack!

After three successful dates, we had agreed to have an overnight stay at a lovely country hotel which I was looking forward to as it would be our first night of intimacy.

On arrival at the hotel and after checking in, I went for a shower only to come out of the room to see restraints attached to the corners of the bed, cuffs and sex toys laid out!

I met up with a guy once from Hinge. I wasn't totally sure about him and the chats were always littered with aubergine emojis and wanting to find out how interested I was in sex, later in life. Against my better judgment I agreed to a date, as he seemed quite witty in between this, and he was 6ft 3in, a rarity. When I arrived at the date, he got very tactile and invaded my personal space, squeezing my knee. He talked incessantly about how sex had dried up with his wife for years and was asking intimate and embarrassing personal questions about my sex life in the middle of a café full of families as it was a Sunday afternoon, so I quickly ended the date. Even as I was leaving he grabbed my bottom as a parting shot. He seemed very surprised when I said no further dates were on the cards.

After matching with someone, the second line after an intro was to say that he was heavily into the swinging scene and only wanted to meet someone and have a relationship if they would go swinging with him. Was that something I'd like? It was a no from me.

I'd had a few drinks. We were sitting across from each other. I fumbled around in my handbag to find my lip gloss. I pulled it out and up to my mouth, only to discover it was a tampon.

I went on a blind date that had been organised by a friend. The date turned out to be really boring, going on about himself and his ex for the entire date without asking one question about me. After the date, I sent a message to my friend to tell her what it had been like and how awful it was, only to find out I had sent it to him by mistake.

In my first week on Bumble, I had exchanged numbers with a guy who seemed quite good fun. He dropped me a message to say we needed a call before we went any further. We spoke as if we were doing a business transaction and there were 4 pillars I had to respect and understand if a date was going to be on the cards.

The first was communication and if I didn't communicate well, there was no point, I assured him that was important to me too. The second was integrity, and that honesty and a good moral compass was essential. I assured him I was of the same mind. The third pillar was family and how important that was and without hesitation, I could agree. So up came the last pillar - SEX! He needed me to know he had a low boredom threshold and in order to date me, he had to be sure I would always make sex interesting and varied. He'd like to see me in bars crossing and uncrossing my legs wearing no knickers as an example. I guess at least honest and upfront, but in this case the 'job' interview was terminated as I wasn't up for telling a total stranger about whether or not I was sexually adventurous.

I went on a date which didn't work out, there was no chemistry. I told them at the end of the date in a polite way that they weren't right for me, but the date was very disgruntled that I didn't want a follow-up date demanding to know what was wrong with them. Later that day I got a call from an unknown number. It was a friend of the first date, asking if I'd like to have a date with them as they knew I was single and their friend had said maybe we would get on!

I was asked by a date to meet them barefoot. He clearly had a foot fetish. Not one I followed up!

After several messages and then subsequent video chats, I agreed to go on a date and he travelled from London to meet me on the South coast where I live. After sitting down for a coffee and saying hello, his opening line was "I think I'm a sociopath". As I do coaching as part of my work, instead of flirting I spent the date going over his childhood traumas.

After finding someone on Hinge who was Irish, with the gift of the gab, said they were intelligent and emotionally intelligent, mentioning several times in the bio what a good kisser they were. He said he was into martial arts and looked trim and fit. We had our video call. Although shorter than I'd normally go for, he looked ok on the call and good conversation can make an average date really change for the better. We decided to meet at a pub halfway between us for an hour over a coffee.

As he arrived and got out of the car, he was both shorter than he'd put on his profile and had a distinct paunch hanging over his trousers. I had been cat-fished. The pub turned out to be brightly lit and rather unwelcoming, so wasn't a particularly romantic environment. Willing to see if the intelligence, emotional intelligence and Irish charm he'd talked of could get past the fact that I didn't find him attractive, I gave it the hour. It was a dull hour! As we finished our drinks, I got up to use the bathroom and upon return said OK, I think I will head off as it's rush hour. He asked directly if I was his type or not. I replied it's been great chatting, but no, probably not. He said he could tell that from my body language (I hadn't leaned in for one of his allegedly good kisses). He jumped up, stomped off to his car, barely holding the door for me, leaving it to drop in my face, then instantly blocked me. A proper hissy fit from a man scorned.

I agreed to go on a date with a fit, skiing, tennis playing German after only a few messages. It turned out he worked quite close to me so it wasn't a difficult arrangement. On arriving at the date it was obvious all of his photos were old. He was completely bald, whereas his photos showed him with a full head of hair. The conversation was stilted and as we'd only planned in a 30-minute coffee, I was able to make my escape. After waiting a further half an hour, I messaged to say that however nice it was to meet, I didn't think there was the connection, and the message was read. He must have had a bruised ego, as about 2 hours later he messaged me as if he hadn't received my message, to say he didn't think the date had gone well, and that he wouldn't be having any further dates with me.

I went on a date with a handsome, intelligent doctor in London, who ticked all the right boxes. The conversation on the date flowed well. About halfway through the date, he leant in for a kiss and I instantly felt like I was under attack from an over eager eel on a spin cycle in the washing machine. This from someone who had put on his profile he was a good kisser (I think this is a brave statement as it's very subjective!). Rather daunted, I got through the rest of the date thinking that was very disappointing. As we left the restaurant and went to say goodbye to get our respective taxis, the same thing happened again, this time with the added bonus of him humping against my leg like a randy teenager making little contented noises. It didn't lead to a second date.

After a first date having an early dinner at an Italian restaurant, and a second date at the cinema, my match seemed to think he could take his foot off the gas. Our dates started to revolve around things he liked or needed to do. Date three was a trip to Costco, date four was bird watching and date five was picking up some furniture that he'd bought on Facebook marketplace and I could help him move it into the back of his car. I decided not to wait to find out what date six was.

I matched with a very handsome, fit, silver fox, who had recently gone on dating apps. We had a video call and he seemed very funny and chatty. As we texted and our date approached, he sent a couple of 'jokes' that referred to 'the back door' which I should have paid more attention to.

Our lunch date arrived, and he talked about himself throughout the meal, telling old fashioned misogynist jokes, mostly derogatory about women. He didn't ask me any questions, but as the meal drew to a close asked if I was adventurous in bed. I dodged the question with a laugh.

With the meal over, he walked me to the car, leant in to kiss me goodbye, and whispered his second question of the date in my ear… "Would I let him take me up the a**e? He'd be gentle!"

I managed to escape and quickly messaged him to say his idea of being adventurous and mine were very different and wished him luck with his search. He definitely needed some coaching on how to woo a lady on the first date!

CHAPTER 12

ALTERNATIVE WAYS TO DATE

So while dating apps do work for some people and couples have been known to fall in love, get married and start families as a result, these apps have also led to a string of unsuccessful dating stories as revealed. While apps tend to be a favourite amongst the younger generation, if you're dating after 40 you might want to consider other options before pinning all your hopes on a swipe.

I have tried to explore other ways to date, and also collected success stories from friends who have met their partners offline.

INTRODUCTIONS FROM FRIENDS AND FAMILY

If you let your friends and family know you're looking to meet new people, they may know someone who is a good match. Sadly, my friends and family have been very unforthcoming, but here's a friend's success story.

"Myself and Jim were set up on a blind date that neither of us wanted to go on. I had been divorced for 2 years, and I'd been dating a man who wasn't treating me very well. A friend said enough is enough. She knew someone who was a friend of her husband's who was going through a divorce. Although she'd only met him a couple of times, she said he's good fun and you need to have some fun so come out on a double date with them. I wasn't keen, but she said what have you got to lose?

I don't know what Jim was told, but he didn't know who he was meeting.

I have a high profile job in television so didn't want any preconceptions. Therefore, he hadn't seen any photos of me. I had seen one photo and thought Jim looked nice enough.

We met at the Hotel Du Vin in Brighton at the bar and when he walked in, I couldn't even look at him. I was nervous, struggling to chat, and he talked at me, to fill in the silence.

As we walked from the bar to the restaurant we had booked to eat at, my friend and her husband strode ahead leaving us to talk.

Jim asked what I did, not recognising me and as I wasn't that interested in him, I told him. Just as I had done this, a hen party came around the corner and recognised me, asking Jim to take photos of me with their group!

After that I decided I could let my hair down and got very merry. I thought I'd just get through the evening, then resolved to enjoy being a single mum and get on with life. After the restaurant we went on to a club where we could dance. As we were walking across the dance floor, he took my hand, and I can only describe it as a jolt of electricity that went through both of us and it was as if the world stood still. We looked at each other and although it sounds crazy, it felt like the universe had thrown us together for a reason and he felt it too. He leant in and kissed me. Forty-five minutes later we came up for air! Our friends were really laughing at us but we have been together ever since.

He lived in Brighton and I lived in Surrey, and we took it really slowly. We saw each other once a week, not really going out but enjoying evenings in, chatting for hours and really getting to know each other. With our individual circumstances we were in no rush to be in a serious relationship. We didn't meet each other's children for nearly a year.

After a year he moved in with me, and three years on, we got married. We have now been together for ten years, with both of us going through very difficult times that we have supported each other through and we are best friends as well as being married.

We love our time together, we laugh all the time although life continues to throw us curve balls.

We look back and know that one night where we went out not expecting anything, gave us everything. There are no rules. No fixed path to meet the perfect person. You meet the right person in the right place at the right time. Go into every experience with an open mind and open heart and no expectations and you may find your perfect partner."

THE GYM

If being healthy is high on your agenda of desirable traits, this is a great place to meet like-minded people.

Here's a success story from a good friend of mine.

"I was single for about two years after my marriage dissolved.

I had tried a dating app and had been out on dates with two guys of initial interest but both a definite mismatch on physically meeting.

I joined a small group training gym in Loughborough, where I lived.

The gym had about 90 members.

After being a member for four months, I noticed David as he had been on the same training session as myself, I hadn't really seen him prior to this as we didn't usually train at the same time.

On this one session, we didn't talk to each other… it was just a quick hello but I knew straight away that I liked him and he interested me. I also knew that I hadn't felt like this about anyone in years and years and to be honest didn't think I would.

David came across as quite quiet and very focused on his training so not inviting any engagement or conversation with me or any of the other gym members.

I learnt later that he was only four months post separation from his wife and family.

I also noticed he was wearing a wedding band. I wasn't aware of his personal situation at that stage so I moved my thoughts on.

Our paths crossed a couple of times at the gym but again no conversation for months.

My feelings weren't changing, if anything I knew I liked him more and more.

It wasn't until a few months later I learnt that David had recently separated from his wife by a friend of a friend and that inspired me to send David a message regarding a coincidental fact between the two of us.

We exchanged a couple of messages but there was no follow up from David at all, he certainly "left me hanging."

I was disappointed but still had hope, as I really liked him and guessed the timing wasn't right for him.

A friend of mine knew that I liked David and that he wasn't showing any interest in me, so she happened to mention it to a friend of hers on a night out and this got back to David.

A few weeks later on Christmas week I received an engaging message from David and it was clear that he was interested in meeting.

I learnt later that David was oblivious to my interest in him.

I also learnt that David had hoped to see me and talk to me at the gym's Christmas party but I hadn't gone.

We arranged our first date on 3rd January for dinner, and it was pretty much instant attraction on both sides and the dates followed thick and fast.

At this stage in our lives having both been in challenging marriages, we were apprehensive.

I was also particularly apprehensive about the age difference between David and I. I was 13 years older but learnt quickly that this was just my concern and not David's.

David was concerned about his difficult personal circumstances with his ex wife, and wanted to make sure that I was comfortable with his situation.

This was all discussed early in the relationship, transparency, open communication and honesty for us both, was and has always been an important ingredient.

Two years after meeting we married.

THE LUNCHTIME BAR OR PUB

I did attempt to go to bars on my own in the evening a couple of times to see if that was one way to meet a potential date. I found it very difficult, as people were either in couples or closely knit groups and as a woman on my own felt slightly lost, very much an oddity and in London, had the danger of looking like an escort searching out a client.

In contrast, a friend shared a story about finding love in a pub at lunchtime whilst out with a girlfriend. The atmosphere is less charged, it's easier to chat and being two of you it's easier to be more sociable.

"After two years of attempting to meet someone through dating apps and a couple of short ill-fated relationships, I had lost faith in finding someone.

My friend and I were out in Liverpool and as it was a sunny day, stumbled across a pub with a beer garden that we had never been into.

As we went into the garden, my friend recognised an old friend of hers she hadn't seen for several years talking to another very handsome, younger guy.

We went over to say hello and I was introduced to his friend Mark. As I looked at his face, there was a jolt of electricity passed between us as our eyes met. I felt really flustered as there was such instant chemistry but as we spent the afternoon chatting I relaxed and it was so good to be enjoying Mark's company.

As the afternoon came to an end, he asked for my number to arrange to see me and I was thrilled.

When it came to the next date, he turned up beautifully dressed and as I looked at him it made me suddenly conscious that he was younger and surely couldn't want to be with me.

We went on the date, chatted as freely as before, enjoying each other's company and I found out he was a pilot, which added to my nerves. Such a glamorous role and one that meant he would be constantly meeting other women. Toward the end of the evening fuelled by wine, I picked up the courage to broach our 10-year age gap and he was stunned. It hadn't even crossed his mind. He thought I was beautiful, stylish, vibrant and fun and he felt he was lucky to be out with me.

It took my breath away and I realised my perceptions of what he was thinking could sabotage what was turning out to be an amazing connection, so I instantly put all concerns to the back of my mind and embraced what was happening in the moment. That was two years ago and we are still going strong."

HIKING GROUPS

As someone who enjoys the outdoors and hiking, I joined a couple of Facebook groups, Adventure Singles, which seemed younger and very looks focussed, and Hiking Buddies UK which seemed a good group of like-minded and aged people. My disadvantage was being Leicestershire based and with most hiking being in places like the Lake District, Yorkshire and Cumbria, the locations didn't really work for me to try.

A friend however, who's based up in Blackpool had more success.

"It all started with a post in the UK Hiking Buddies Facebook group. I had joined the group a few months earlier, hoping to find fellow outdoor enthusiasts to explore the stunning trails of the UK. One evening, while scrolling through the feed, I saw a post that caught my eye. Someone named Alex had shared an open invitation for a weekend hike in the Lake District. The plan was ambitious but appealing—Scafell Pike followed by a scenic loop around Buttermere.

I didn't know anyone in the group personally, and the thought of showing up to a hike with strangers was daunting.

I commented on the post, asking about the logistics, and Alex quickly replied with detailed yet friendly instructions. I decided to push myself out of my comfort zone and join.

When Saturday came, I arrived at the trailhead, scanning the group for any familiar faces from the profile pictures I'd seen. Alex waved me over with a big smile, instantly making me feel welcome. Their energy was infectious, and I found it was really easy to chat albeit the group separated slightly walking at different paces as we began the ascent.

The hike was breathtaking. The crisp mountain air, the rolling green hills, and the camaraderie of the group made it unforgettable.

As the group spread out, more and more often, Alex and I found ourselves walking side by side, sharing stories about our favourite hikes, a shared passion for travel and adventures, including a dream to go to the Galapagos Islands. Not many people match my energy for life and it was nice to meet someone who did.

By the time we reached the summit of Scafell Pike,

it felt like I'd known Alex for years. We took a group photo, but we got a couple of selfies together as it would be a good memory to have.

After the hike, a smaller group of us decided to grab a bite at a nearby pub. Over post-hike burgers and beers, Alex and I ended up sitting next to each other. I was conscious of our knees touching. Before we left, Alex asked if I'd be interested in joining them for another hike the following weekend. I said yes without hesitation.

That next hike turned into coffee dates, which turned into dinner dates, which eventually turned into us officially dating.

I never imagined I'd find my partner, someone who shares my love for the outdoors. I would highly recommend it to anyone who loves hiking and wants to meet someone similar."

A few more ideas to consider, all of which I tried...

SALSA LESSONS

I had fun here and learned to salsa. There was a mix of single people and couples and the nature of the dance and the lessons mean that you rotate around different partners.

PROFESSIONAL NETWORKING EVENTS

If you go to these, you are meeting up with a select group of people who are in a similar demographic to you and may have similar lifestyles. I know I am not alone to have had approaches via LinkedIn asking for a date via messages. It seems every platform can be a dating platform if you make it that way!

SOCIAL MEDIA

Being an Instagram user, it is possible to follow friends of friends and I have certainly made some great female Insta friends but have also been asked on a couple of coffee dates with men who I have connected with via the app.

ART CLASSES

I signed up for life drawing classes accompanied by my girlfriend and it was a great way to meet new people with similar interests. I am yet to find romance, but it's certainly a very easy way to chat to someone in a relaxed environment, so who knows?

SOLO HOLIDAYS

I tried my first solo holiday aged 61 focussing on watercolour painting and loved it. The group I went with was predominantly women so not conducive to meeting a partner, but it built my confidence, I made new friends. I am currently looking at booking another solo holiday that will have a more mixed clientele, so watch this space.

CHAPTER 13
MY SURVIVAL GUIDE SUMMARY

1 **Spend time dating yourself first.** Practice self-love first and you will be ready to re-enter the dating game happier, more confident and comfortable in your own skin. All very dateable qualities!

2 **Be clear what you want from your next relationship, your needs and desires.** Know your non-negotiables and where you are flexible. It will make you stronger and more decisive on your dating journey.

3 **Take the time to define what you seek in a partner.** Have your shopping list but be prepared to stay open-minded. I had some of my best dates when I broadened my view of what I wanted.

4 **Take time over your online dating profile.** This is your chance to present yourself in all your fabulous, unique glory. In the dating market, this is your chance to advertise yourself! Your first photo will be the hook in this very visual world, but for those men that seek a bit more depth and read your profile, be your best self. Remember, be authentic. If you aren't right for them, they are not right for you.

5 **Use profile relevant, open questions to find out more about your potential date.** As a rule of thumb, if I asked all the questions, and they weren't curious about me, they didn't get past go. If someone is interested in finding out more about you (without asking for your bank details!) it means they are seeing past just your looks and want to find out more about you as a person. This is a good sign.

6 I'd highly recommend that if you are enjoying a conversation on text, rather than investing your time and energy in several days worth of endless texting, have a video call in the app. You can quickly assess whether you can have a conversation in real life and that the person does look like their photos.

7 Engage in meaningful conversations to see if this is someone who meets your needs and desires. If the conversation gets sexualised very quickly don't feel forced to reciprocate. Have clear boundaries and if they are overstepped, this date is not for you.

8 Use the three date rule. If it's not an obvious no on the first date, but you are not sure, have a second date. Nerves or shyness can sometimes get in the way the first time you meet for both parties, so giving the match a second chance may lead to a more successful date. If there's still no chemistry or connection after a third date, it's probably never going to happen.

9 Trust your instincts. If something feels too good to be true, it probably is.

10 With only 1/3 of marriages coming from online dating, that means 2/3 aren't. Be open to exploring different avenues to meet new people. It may mean pushing yourself out of your comfort zone but even if you don't meet a date, you will have had new experiences, maybe made new friends or like me have some corking stories to tell your friends.

LASTLY, REMEMBER THIS IS SUPPOSED TO BE FUN!

Even if your goal is to meet a long-term life partner or future husband, if you overthink or plan too far into the future, you may not make the most of enjoying the journey. I am still laughing about the interesting conversations, both as a result of my good dates and my bad dates.

You can reframe the journey as an exciting adventure. Embrace the present moment and allow yourself to have fun.

GO WITH THE FLOW

Overthinking about the future will make this process feel like a chore and we have enough of those in our lives!

Overanalysing whether someone ticks every box will detract from the joy of simply getting to know them.

Live in the moment instead of asking "Are they the one?" Do you or your date want to feel scrutinised through the lens of future expectations instead of feeling genuinely appreciated?

REVEL IN THE JOY OF DISCOVERY

Embrace each date as an opportunity to learn about someone's unique quirks, passions, and perspectives, even if romance doesn't blossom you may make a new friend. Enjoy meeting someone new without being bogged down by worries about where the relationship might lead. Love doesn't have a plan or a deadline, it's more likely to creep up on us when we're least expecting it, while we're busy living and enjoying the journey.

Go into each date filled with curiosity and open to have fun.

You're more likely to relax and be yourself. And that's the person, the wonderful, quirky, individual, fabulous you, they may fall in love with.

SO HAVE I GOT A HAPPY ENDING?

As I write this, I'm still single, I'm still sassy and I am now more than 60. I am VERY happy with being that. Whether I end up in a relationship or not, 40, 50, 60 or 70 is no barrier to getting back on the dating scene. What I have discovered is that there's no rush. I don't need someone to complete me.

Live your best life, live in the moment and love yourself. That's the best date you're going to have.